Mastering Hibernate

Learn how to correctly utilize the most popular
Object-Relational Mapping tool for your
Enterprise application

Ramin Rad

BIRMINGHAM - MUMBAI

Mastering Hibernate

First published: May 2016

Production reference: 1100516

Published by Packt Publishing Ltd.
Livery Place
35 Livery Street
Birmingham B3 2PB, UK.

ISBN 978-1-78217-533-9

www.packtpub.com

Credits

Author
Ramin Rad

Reviewers
Luca Masini

Sherwin John Calleja-Tragura

Aurélie Vache

Commissioning Editor
Neil Alexander

Acquisition Editor
Reshma Raman

Content Development Editor
Zeeyan Pinheiro

Technical Editor
Pranjali Mistry

Copy Editor
Pranjali Chury

Project Coordinator
Francina Pinto

Proofreader
Safis Editing

Indexer
Rekha Nair

Production Coordinator
Manu Joseph

Cover Work
Manu Joseph

About the Author

Ramin Rad has been working as a software professional for the last 20 years, living in Washington DC area. He studied mathematics and computer science in the academic world, and he cares deeply for the art of software development.

He is also a musician, a guitarist, who performs regularly in the DC area and beyond. His artistic side is significant because he believes that writing software is more art than science, following the philosophy of the likes of Donald Knuth, who wrote the *Art of Computer Programming* series.

Currently, he is a director and a solution architect at a large international software product and services company, focusing on enterprise, mobile, and cloud-based solutions.

I would like to thank three people who have made a significant impact on my professional life and career: my friend, Terry Rice, who always encouraged me to think scientifically and redirect my focus toward software architecture; my idol, Dr. Paul Eggert, who for me is a true computer scientist and with whom I had the pleasure of working; and finally my mentor, Jon King, who has guided me the most throughout my career and personal life.

Finally, I dedicate this book to my beautiful children, Mina and Cyrus. I hope when you grow up, you too love and learn all about life, nature, and science, and share what you learn with the world.

About the Reviewers

Luca Masini is a senior software engineer and architect. He started off as a game developer for Commodore 64 (Football Manager) and Commodore Amiga (Ken il guerriero). He soon converted to object oriented programming, and for that, from its beginning in 1995, he was attracted by the Java language.

Following his passion, he worked as a consultant for major Italian banks, developing and integrating the main software projects for which he has often taken technical leadership. He encouraged the adoption Java Enterprise in environments where COBOL was the flagship platform, converting them from mainframe centric to distributed.

He then shifted his focus toward open source, starting from Linux and then moving to enterprise frameworks with which he was able to introduce concepts such as IoC, ORM, and MVC with low impact. For that, he was an early adopter of Spring, Hibernate, Struts, and a whole host of other technologies that in the long run have given his customers a technological advantage and, therefore, development cost reduction.

After introducing new technology, he decided that it was time for simplification and standardization of development with Java EE, and as such, he's now working in the ICT of a large Italian company, where he has introduced build tools (Maven and continuous integration), archetypes of project, and agile development with plain standards.

Finally, he has focused his attention on mobilizing the enterprise and is now working on a whole set of standard and development processes to introduce mobile concepts and applications for sales force and management.

He has worked on the following books by Packt Publishing:

- *Securing WebLogic Server 12c*
- *Google Web Toolkit*
- *Spring Web Flow 2*
- *Spring Persistence with Hibernate*
- *Spring Batch Essentials*
- *Spring Integration Essentials*

Sherwin John Calleja-Tragura has been a software consultant, technical trainer, and software analyst specializing in Java/JEE and Android specification. He started his career as a lecturer and numerical analyst at the University of the Philippines, Los Baños (UPLB), emphasizing on optimization of linear algorithms. In 2006, he became one of the Documentum and Alfresco consultants at Ayala Systems and Technology Inc. (ASTI) in Manila, Philippines. Currently, he is a technical consultant at Alibata Solutions and Technology Services Inc. and a Java/JEE technical trainer at Software Laboratory Inc. (SLI).

He has technically edited books such as *Delphi Cookbook,*,*Alfresco 3 Records Management*, and *Alfresco Share*, all by Packt Publishing.

He has taken 30 course units of masters of science in the computer science curriculum of UPLB.

I would like to thank my grandmother, Lila Calleja, for the continuous support and prayers for the success of all my work and my father, Cesar Tragura, for his encouragement and perseverance. I'd also like to thank Owen Salvador Estabillo, Matthew Jeoffrey Domino, Mark Joseph Ikang Fernandez, and Rostan Valdez for building my confidence and boosting my morale.

Aurélie Vache is a full-stack developer, working for atchikservices in Toulouse, France. She has been working as a developer for over 10 years.

A former Java/JEE developer, she has been developing business and social apps, backend and frontends services, websites, and lead technical projects. She has also been giving attention to UX and SEO, managing QoS (quality of service), and deploying apps in production for several years now. She is also a DevOps and enjoys Big Data technologies.

As a Duchess France Leader, she is strongly involved with Duchess France (`www.duchess-france.org`), an association promoting women developers and women in IT, inspiring and encouraging them to speak at conferences or technical events. The Duchess France team has launched a new coaching initiative (#AdoptADuchess) in order to help junior devlopers.

You can meet her at meetups in Toulouse, specifically at JUG, DevOps, and Toulouse Data Science, where she has already talked about Google BigQuery, the Big Data analytics as a service (AaaS) Google technology.

A couple of months ago, she was a member of the jury for the Senat (French Senate) IT developer contest in order to recruit two developers in the Information Systems Department (ISD).

www.PacktPub.com

eBooks, discount offers, and more

Did you know that Packt offers eBook versions of every book published, with PDF and ePub files available? You can upgrade to the eBook version at www.PacktPub.com and as a print book customer, you are entitled to a discount on the eBook copy. Get in touch with us at customercare@packtpub.com for more details.

At www.PacktPub.com, you can also read a collection of free technical articles, sign up for a range of free newsletters and receive exclusive discounts and offers on Packt books and eBooks.

https://www2.packtpub.com/books/subscription/packtlib

Do you need instant solutions to your IT questions? PacktLib is Packt's online digital book library. Here, you can search, access, and read Packt's entire library of books.

Why subscribe?

- Fully searchable across every book published by Packt
- Copy and paste, print, and bookmark content
- On demand and accessible via a web browser

Table of Contents

Preface

Object-Relational Mapping is a difficult problem, and the Hibernate team has solved that problem for us. Some developers have a love-hate relationship with Hibernate because it has made life easier for many developers, but at times, unexpected behavior is encountered and it quickly becomes a mystery. This book was written to uncover these mysteries. It does so by looking under the hood; it first discusses the internals of Hibernate, and later it covers advanced topics on mapping techniques, annotations, fetching, caching, and versioning. It also addresses other topics that are of interest to technical leads and software architects, such as statistics and metrics, concurrency, and transaction management.

Although, it is recommended that you read this book in its entirety, the topics are carefully outlined so that it can also be used as a reference if you wish to learn about a specific feature.

What this book covers

Chapter 1, Entity and Session, covers the internal working of a session and how Hibernate manages entities inside a session. We will also explore the entity life cycle and discuss other topics related to sessions and entities such as stateless sessions, design patterns such as session-per-request, session-per-conversation, batch processing, and proxy objects.

Chapter 2, Advanced Mapping, talks about fundamental mapping concepts and how Hibernate bridges the gap between the object-oriented world and relational database. You will further read discussions on inheritance, and in-memory and in-database value generation. Moreover, the creation of custom mapped data types is also covered. This chapter also demonstrates how to work with collections and offers tips and tricks, and outlines the pitfalls when working with collections. Additionally, it covers batch updates and deletes. Finally, this chapter shows you how to implement object-oriented topics such as inheritance and polymorphism and map them correctly to a relational database.

Chapter 3, Working with Annotations, demonstrates the use of annotations and why and when to use them. Besides the common annotations, it highlights some rare ones, which can be quite useful for most developers. In addition to the common JPA annotations, this chapter also discusses some annotations that are only available in Hibernate.

Chapter 4, Advanced Fetching, shows various fetching strategies and discusses the use of Hibernate and native query languages, criteria objects, filters, and other topics related to data fetch.

Chapter 5, Hibernate Cache, covers various cache structures such as first-level and second-level. Additionally, it explores various cache strategies and how to collect statistics related to caching.

Chapter 6, Events, Interceptors, and Envers, covers events and interceptors in Hibernate and how you can use them to implement a functionality similar to DB triggers and other event-based functions. Furthermore, it covers Entity Auditing (Envers); which implements entity revision management to automatically store historical snapshots of entities and also provides an auditing mechanism.

Chapter 7, Metrics and Statistics, demonstrates how to generate and collect metrics and statistical data within Hibernate. This includes entity, query, collection, and cache statistics. It further shows how to access this data via JMX, that is, Java Management Extensions.

Chapter 8, Addressing Architecture, shows how architectural concerns and constraints are addressed in Hibernate, which includes concurrency and transaction management, scalability, and performance.

Chapter 9, EJB and Spring Context, shows how to correctly create and deploy your application in two popular Java contexts, EJB and Spring.

What you need for this book

All the code in this book is written using Java SE 7. You will need a Java IDE (Integrated Development Environment) such as Eclipse, Netbeans, or IntelliJ. Additionally, you will need a relational database, such as Oracle, DB2, MySQL, or PostgreSQL. The database used to create the examples in this book is PostgreSQL database (version 9.3).

Most of the examples in the initial chapters are single-threaded Java applications that do not need to run inside a Java Enterprise container or Spring. However, in later chapters, you will need to test your enterprise application in a container. In this case, JBoss (AS 7) or Spring (version 4.2) were chosen.

Although, you may not need it, it is highly recommended that you use a dependency manager for your work. The examples in this book use Apache Maven, version 3.

Who this book is for

This book covers fundamental concepts of Hibernate. It is intended for highly technical developers who wish to understand the internals of Hibernate. This book can also be used by developers who have already started using Hibernate and wish to get better at it. It is not intended to make you a Java or SQL developer. If you wish to learn about the how and why, then this book is for you. Mastery is about details.

Conventions

In this book, you will find a number of text styles that distinguish between different kinds of information. Here are some examples of these styles and an explanation of their meaning.

Code words in text, database table names, folder names, filenames, file extensions, pathnames, dummy URLs, user input, and Twitter handles are shown as follows: "The @Any and @ManyToAny annotations are only available in Hibernate."

A block of code is set as follows:

```
@Entity
public class Person {
@Id
@GeneratedValue
private long id;
private String firstname;
private String lastname;
```

```
private String ssn;
private Date birthdate;
// getters and setters
}
```

When we wish to draw your attention to a particular part of a code block, the relevant lines or items are set in bold:

```
{
Entity
public class Circle {
@Id
@GeneratedValue
}
}
```

Any command-line input or output is written as follows:

```
select
course0_.id as id1_0_0_,
course0_.title as title2_0_0_,
students1_.course_id as course_i4_0_1_,
students1_.id as id1_1_1_,
students1_.gender as gender2_1_2_,
students1_.name as name3_1_2_
from
Course course0_
```

 Warnings or important notes appear in a box like this.

 Tips and tricks appear like this.

Reader feedback

Feedback from our readers is always welcome. Let us know what you think about this book—what you liked or disliked. Reader feedback is important for us as it helps us develop titles that you will really get the most out of.

To send us general feedback, simply e-mail feedback@packtpub.com, and mention the book's title in the subject of your message.

If there is a topic that you have expertise in and you are interested in either writing or contributing to a book, see our author guide at www.packtpub.com/authors.

Customer support

Now that you are the proud owner of a Packt book, we have a number of things to help you to get the most from your purchase.

Downloading the example code

You can download the example code files for this book from your account at http://www.packtpub.com. If you purchased this book elsewhere, you can visit http://www.packtpub.com/support and register to have the files e-mailed directly to you.

You can download the code files by following these steps:

1. Log in or register to our website using your e-mail address and password.
2. Hover the mouse pointer on the **SUPPORT** tab at the top.
3. Click on **Code Downloads & Errata**.
4. Enter the name of the book in the **Search** box.
5. Select the book for which you're looking to download the code files.
6. Choose from the drop-down menu where you purchased this book from.
7. Click on **Code Download**.

You can also download the code files by clicking on the **Code Files** button on the book's webpage at the Packt Publishing website. This page can be accessed by entering the book's name in the **Search** box. Please note that you need to be logged in to your Packt account.

Once the file is downloaded, please make sure that you unzip or extract the folder using the latest version of:

- WinRAR / 7-Zip for Windows
- Zipeg / iZip / UnRarX for Mac
- 7-Zip / PeaZip for Linux

Errata

Although we have taken every care to ensure the accuracy of our content, mistakes do happen. If you find a mistake in one of our books—maybe a mistake in the text or the code—we would be grateful if you could report this to us. By doing so, you can save other readers from frustration and help us improve subsequent versions of this book. If you find any errata, please report them by visiting http://www.packtpub.com/submit-errata, selecting your book, clicking on the **Errata Submission Form** link, and entering the details of your errata. Once your errata are verified, your submission will be accepted and the errata will be uploaded to our website or added to any list of existing errata under the Errata section of that title.

To view the previously submitted errata, go to https://www.packtpub.com/books/content/support and enter the name of the book in the search field. The required information will appear under the **Errata** section.

Piracy

Piracy of copyrighted material on the Internet is an ongoing problem across all media. At Packt, we take the protection of our copyright and licenses very seriously. If you come across any illegal copies of our works in any form on the Internet, please provide us with the location address or website name immediately so that we can pursue a remedy.

Please contact us at copyright@packtpub.com with a link to the suspected pirated material.

We appreciate your help in protecting our authors and our ability to bring you valuable content.

Questions

If you have a problem with any aspect of this book, you can contact us at questions@packtpub.com, and we will do our best to address the problem.

1
Entity and Session

In this chapter, we will take an in-depth look at sessions and entities and their lifecycles. It is important to understand the concepts of session and entity when we talk about design concepts, such as session-per-request, session-per-conversation, stateless sessions, and contextual sessions, and discuss the various states of an entity. After all, the only way to master anything is by paying attention to the details. We also explore entities beyond their JPA characteristics and look at Hibernate entities to see the benefits of one over the other. Furthermore, we discuss proxy objects and how they are used.

In this chapter, we will cover the following topics:

- Why this book?
- Quick Hibernate
- Hibernate session:
    - Session internals
    - Contextual sessions
    - Sessions per request, per conversation, and per operation
    - Stateless sessions
- Hibernate entities:
    - Entity lifecycle
    - Types of entities
    - Identity crisis
    - Beyond JPA
- Proxy objects

- Batch processing:
  - Manual batch management
  - Setting the size of the batch

- Using a stateless session

Why this book?

Java developers solve problems using object-oriented concepts. We design applications using classes to model business entities. Furthermore, we utilize inheritance to imply that a class is another kind of class, or is composed of primitive fields and other classes, and visualize the application data as objects or object graphs. However, we also have a persistence problem.

Traditionally, the storage unit is implemented using structured records (tuples), which are stored in tables (relations) that may or may not be associated with each other. This concept is supported by a declarative language, which is limited in scope and is primarily for data creation and data manipulation. Tuples and objects have a lot in common; they both have attributes (columns and fields), and the attributes have data types (int, char, and so on), but the persistence problem becomes evident when you look at the differences between tuples and objects, such as identity, equality, or inheritance.

Object-Relational Mapping is a hard problem. Luckily, Hibernate makes this easy. You probably discovered this by reading the first few chapters of the Hibernate online documents or another book; and as you have to meet tight deadlines, you reactively solve your problems when they surface by swiftly paging through a book, searching or posting on *stackoverflow,* or other online forums or blogs. You spent half a day trying to find your answer and then moved on until the next problem surfaced. I have done it, you have done it; we *ALL* do it.

However, what if you knew about the internals of Hibernate and how it works? You wouldn't need to know everything about Hibernate, but you would know exactly where to look quickly to find your answer, such as a dictionary.

This book was written to explore the fundamental concepts of Hibernate and discuss them in detail, so that next time you run into a problem, you can identify the issue and find the answer that you want quickly. For example, whether a problem is a mapping problem or just improper use of an annotation. Furthermore, you will design better software once you understand the internals of any framework that you decide to use.

The main objectives of this book are to help you understand Hibernate beyond the basics, make you appreciate the ORM problem, and show you why Hibernate is one of the best solutions that exists today. We focus more on the Hibernate API and occasionally explore the JPA counterpart. This book assumes that you have a basic understanding of Hibernate and have used it in the past, or you are currently using it. If this is not the case for you, please visit the Hibernate documentation online, as it offers guides to get started with Hibernate and more.

Quick Hibernate

In this section, we take a glance at a typical Hibernate application and its components. Hibernate is designed to work in a standalone application as well as a Java Enterprise application, such as a Web or EJB application. All topics discussed here are covered in detail throughout this book.

The standalone version of a Hibernate application is comprised of the components that are shown in the following figure:

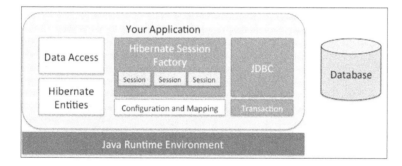

We, the application developers, create the components that are depicted by the white boxes, namely the data access classes, entity classes, and configuration and mapping. Everything else is provided in form of a JAR or a runtime environment.

The Hibernate session factory is responsible for creating a session when your application requests it. The factory is configured using the configuration files that you provide. Some of the configuration settings are used for JDBC parameters, such as database username, password, and connection URL. Other parameters are used to modify the behavior of a session and the factory.

You may already be familiar with the configuration file that looks like the following:

```xml
<hibernate-configuration>
    <session-factory>
        <property name="connection.driver_class">
            org.postgresql.Driver
        </property>
        <property name="connection.url">
            jdbc:postgresql://localhost:5432/packtdb
        </property>
        <property name="connection.username">user</property>
        <property name="connection.password">pass</property>
        <property name="connection.pool_size">1</property>
        <property name="dialect">
            org.hibernate.dialect.PostgreSQLDialect
        </property>
        <property name="current_session_context_class">
            thread
        </property>
        <property name="show_sql">true</property>
        <property name="format_sql">true</property>
    </session-factory>
</hibernate-configuration>
```

The initialization of the session factory has changed slightly in the newer versions of Hibernate. You now have to use a service registry, as shown here:

```java
private static SessionFactory buildSessionFactory() {
    try {
     // Create the SessionFactory from hibernate.cfg.xml
     // in resources directory
      Configuration configuration = new Configuration()
        .configure()
        .addAnnotatedClass(Person.class);
      StandardServiceRegistryBuilder builder =
        new StandardServiceRegistryBuilder()
        .applySettings(configuration.getProperties());
      serviceRegistry = builder.build();
      return configuration
        .buildSessionFactory(serviceRegistry);
    }
    catch (Throwable ex) {
        // do something with the exception
        throw new ExceptionInInitializerError(ex);
    }
}
```

The data objects are represented by Hibernate entities. A simple Hibernate entity, which uses annotation, is shown here:

```
@Entity
public class Person {
  @Id
  @GeneratedValue
  private long id;
  private String firstname;
  private String lastname;
  private String ssn;
  private Date birthdate;
  // getters and setters
}
```

The last component that we have to create is the data access class, which is the service that provides the **Create, Read, Update, Delete (CRUD)** operations for entities. An example of storing an entity is shown here:

```
Session session = HibernateUtil.getSessionFactory()
  .getCurrentSession();
Transaction transaction = session.beginTransaction();

try {
 Person person = new Person();
 person.setFirstname("John");
 person.setLastname("Williams");
 person.setBirthdate(randomBirthdate());
 person.setSsn(randomSsn());
  session.save(person);
  transaction.commit();
} catch (Exception e) {
  transaction.rollback();
  e.printStackTrace();
} finally {
  if (session.isOpen())
    session.close();
}
```

That's it!

The Java Enterprise application doesn't look very different from the standalone version. The difference is mainly in the application stack and where each component resides, as shown in the following diagram:

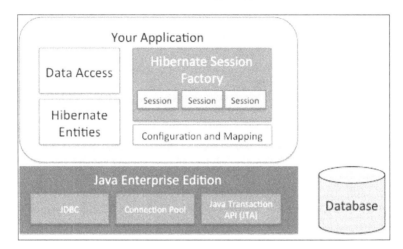

This example provides a context of what we will discuss in detail throughout this book. Let's begin by taking a closer look at a Hibernate session.

Working with a session

The core operations of Hibernate occur in the session. This is where connection to the database is obtained, **Structured Query Language (SQL)** statements are composed, type conversions are made, and where transactions and the persistence context are managed. Let's start by getting to know the internals of a Hibernate session.

Session internals

If you have written at least one Hibernate application in the past, you already know what an entity and a session are. However, most of the time, developers don't think about the session, the entity, and their lifecycles, or about what occurs inside a session when an entity is saved or updated. There are fundamental concepts that one must understand in order to utilize Hibernate effectively.

The Hibernate session is where persistence work is performed for each thread of execution, and it manages the *persistence context*. Therefore, it's not thread-safe; this means that multiple threads should not access or use the same session at the same time. As you may know, sessions are created by calling the session factory, and there is only one factory per storage unit, although you can have multiple session factories pointing to different databases.

Furthermore, the session is designed to be a short-lived object. This is an important constraint that is typically imposed by the database and the application server, and this is because there is always a timeout setting on connections and transactions. (There is even timeout setting at the **Java Database Connectivity (JDBC)** level. Furthermore, you have to worry about TCP Socket timeout.) Even though these settings are set to some number of seconds, you should still avoid long-running logics while the session is open because you may create contention in the database and impact the system performance altogether. Hibernate tries to protect you by not allocating any resources, such as database connections, unless they are absolutely needed. However, you still have to be mindful of the work that you do within the unit of persistence work. As long as you limit the code to persistence-related tasks while you have an open session, you will be fine.

When you create a session factory, Hibernate reads the configuration file and, at first, loads the SQL `dialect` class. This class includes a mapping for the database types and operations for the specific **Relational Database Management System (RDBMS)** server, which you work with. Hibernate then adds all these types, as well as the user-defined types to a type resolver. (You will learn about creating custom types in *Chapter 2*, *Advanced Mapping*.)

Additionally, when a session factory is created, Hibernate loads all the entities that are added to the configuration. You can add annotated entities to the configuration in the code, or create an entity mapping file and add the entity map to the configuration file. For each entity, Hibernate precomposes the JDBC-prepared SQL statements for `select`, `insert`, `update`, and `delete`. (This also creates one to support entity versioning, refer to the *Envers* section, in *Chapter 6*, *Events, Interceptors, and Envers*). This is called a static SQL. Some entity types require a dynamic SQL, for example, dynamic entities.

Hibernate also creates internal maps for each entity property and its association with other entities and collections. This is because Hibernate uses reflection to access properties or to invoke methods on your entity. In addition to the entity properties, Hibernate also keeps track of all the annotations that are associated with properties and methods so that it can perform certain operations when needed, such as cascade operations.

When you obtain a session object from the factory, you may get a different implementation of the `CurrentSessionContext` interface, depending on the session context class. There are three session contexts that are natively supported: **Java Transaction API (JTA)**, thread, and managed contexts. This is set using the `current_session_context_class` configuration parameter, and Hibernate has reserved the shortcuts, `jta`, `managed`, and `thread`, to expand to the corresponding internal classes. However, you can replace this with any class, which implements `org.hibernate.context.spi.CurrentSessionContext`.

Starting with version 4, Hibernate has repackaged the classes to follow the OSGi model for more modular, pluggable, and extensible applications and frameworks. Many of the named resources, such as dialect and connection provider, are now managed through services. Services have a lifecycle (initialize, start, and stop), a rich callback API, and provide support for JMX and CDI, among others. There are three main packages in Hibernate, the API packages, the SPI packages, and the internal packages. The classes in the API packages are the ones that we utilize to use Hibernate. The classes in the **Service Provider Interface** (**SPI**) are pluggable modules that are typically replaced or provided by vendors who want to implement or override certain components of Hibernate. Finally, the classes in the internal packages are used internally by Hibernate. We will come back to this in *Chapter 6, Events, Interceptors, and Envers*, when we discuss events.

Transaction management means different things for the internal session contexts. This is an important architectural discussion, which will be covered in detail in *Chapter 8, Addressing Architecture*. However, in the next section, we will discuss contextual sessions, and for this, we need to define session scope and transaction boundaries.

The persistence unit of work begins when you start a new session. Hibernate will not allow modification to the persistence context without an active transaction. You either begin a local transaction (in the JDBC session context), or one is started by JTA or the managed context. The unit of persistence work ends when you commit or rollback a transaction. This also closes the session automatically, assuming that the default is not overridden. If you start a local transaction and don't commit it or roll back, Hibernate quietly clears the persistence context when you close the session. If you don't close the session after your work is done, you will most definitely have a connection leak. (This behavior varies for different session contexts.)

When you call various methods on the session object, these methods are translated into a corresponding event. For example, the `session.save()` method is translated into an instance of the `SaveOrUpdateEvent` class, and the actual operations are managed by event listeners. Each session has a list of event listeners, which perform certain operations for each event that is fired off in the execution path. As another example, when you check to see whether the session is dirty, `session.isDirty()`, a `DirtyCheckEvent` event, is fired off to check the action queue to see whether any actions are queued up, and if so, it marks the session as dirty.

So what is the action queue? Most Hibernate events correspond to one or more actions. Each session has an instance of the `ActionQueue` class that holds a list of various actions. These actions are simple `insert`, `delete`, and `update` actions on entities and collections. While you are working within a session and updating the persistence context, actions get queued up as various events are fired. Finally, at the end of the transaction, on commit, these actions are translated into **Data Manipulation Language (DML)** statements by the corresponding `entity persister` classes (for example, `SingleTableEntityPersister`), which are then executed in the database. (The composition of the SQL statements is managed by classes in the `org.hibernate.sql` package, which use the dialect classes to form a syntactically correct SQL statement.)

This is basically what happens inside a Hibernate session from the time it is created until it is closed. Next, we will discuss various session contexts and how they differ.

What is the difference between a session and an entity manager?

Session is the Hibernate API to manage the persistence context. Entity manager is its counterpart in the JPA world. Although new versions of Hibernate implement the JPA specifications, you still have a choice to use Hibernate or JPA APIs. Your code is fully portable if you choose the JPA APIs, regardless of the implementation. On the other hand, you will have more control if you choose the Hibernate API.

Isn't the session the same as the persistence context?

No. Besides doing a lot of other things, the session also manages the persistence context, which happens to be its main job. Think of the persistence context as your copy of the database rows in memory, managed by the session. (Obviously, these are only the rows that you are working with.)

Contextual session

The session behaves differently in various contexts. This behavior is defined in terms of session scope, transaction boundaries, and the cleanup work. As mentioned earlier, there are three types of contextual sessions that are natively supported by Hibernate. These are as follows:

- `JTASessionContext`
- `ThreadLocalSessionContext`
- `ManagedSessionContext`

All of these implement the `CurrentSessionContext` interface. Simply put, the context defines the scope of the current session.

The scope of JTA session context is defined by the transaction that is being managed by JTA. In this case, the current session is bound to the JTA transaction and, therefore, the cleanup is triggered by JTA when lifecycle events are fired off. Once the transaction is committed, the session is flushed, cleared, and then closed. If your application runs in an environment where a transaction manager is deployed, you should always use this context.

The scope of thread local session context is defined by the current thread. This context is best suitable for unit tests or standalone applications, as it is not meant for usage in an enterprise application. In this case, the current session is bound to the current thread and the transaction that you start comes straight from JDBC. If you use the Hibernate transaction API (that is `Transaction transaction = session.beginTransaction();`), and you should, it will perform the cleanup for you.

The scope of the managed session context is somewhat defined by the current thread, but the scope can expand over multiple threads. In this case, the session outlives the thread that created it and may be flushed and closed by a subsequent thread. In other words, you are defining the scope of the session, and you have to manually handle cleanup work. You are managing the session.

What does flush do?

When you modify the persistence context by adding new entities, or updating the existing one, the database and persistence context are not synchronized until the end of persistence work. Only after `flush()` is called, changes to Hibernate entities are propagated to the corresponding tables and rows. Hibernate offers very powerful capabilities to manage flush behavior when this synchronization actually occurs. You will see more on this later.

In other words, when you call the `getCurrentSession` of the Hibernate session factory API, the behavior is as follows:

- `thread`: This session factory API returns the current session that is associated with the current thread. (If one doesn't exist, this will create one and associate it with the current thread.)
- `jta`: This session factory API returns the current session that is associated with the current global transaction. In case of none, one is created and associated with the current global transaction through JTA.

- managed: You'll have to use ManagedSessionContext to obtain the correct session for the current thread. This is useful when you want to call multiple data access classes and don't want to pass the session object to each class. Refer to the following discussion on session per operation.

The JTA and threadlocal session contexts might be what you are used to and are easier to understand. The Managed session context is best for long-running conversations that represent a business unit of work, which spans multiple requests. If this sounds a bit cryptic, do not worry; we will come back to this later on.

Session per request

In this design pattern, all the persistence work for each client request is accomplished within one session. If all the business transactions within a unit of work can be encapsulated in one **Data Access Object (DAO)** implementation, then you can start a session and a transaction at the beginning of your method, and commit at the end. (Don't forget proper exception handling!)

If your business unit of work spans multiple DAO classes, then you have to make sure that they all use the same session. Hibernate makes this easy for you by providing the sessionFactory.getCurrentSession() API. This will allow you to access the session object from anywhere within the same thread.

However, here's the catch. You need to make sure that somebody has started the transaction whose commit and rollback is also delegated appropriately. This can be orchestrated in a service method, where you can start a Hibernate session, begin transaction, and store the session object in a static ThreadLocal session, or pass the session object to each DAO instance, either as constructor argument or passed directly to each method. Once the orchestration is completed, you can commit the transaction.

If you use EJBs, you are in luck! You simply wire EntityManager and declare a DAO method transactional using the @TransactionAttribute annotation, and the EJB container will take care of the rest for you. We will demonstrate this, and another elegant solution using Spring, in *Chapter 9, EJB and Spring Context*.

Session per conversation

This pattern is used when the business transaction spans over multiple units of persistence work, and the business data is exchanged over multiple consecutive requests with allowed think time in between.

In a sense, the DAO orchestration that we discussed earlier implements this pattern. However, in that case, everything occurred in one client request (one thread of execution): the session was opened, the transaction started, DAO methods were called, the session was flushed and cleared, the transaction was committed, the response was sent to the client, and the thread ended. This is not considered a long-running conversation.

When implementing session per conversation, as the name indicates, the session scope goes beyond a single thread and a single database transaction. This is why a managed session context is best for this pattern. You can control flush behavior so that synchronization doesn't occur until you are ready to perform it.

In order to understand how this works, we need an in-depth understanding of entity lifecycle and transactions. There are various ways of implementing this pattern, and we will cover these later in this book.

Session per operation

This is considered an anti-pattern. It's true that the instantiation of the session object is not expensive, but managing the persistence context and allocating or obtaining connection and transaction resources is expensive. If your business transaction is comprised of multiple persistence operations, you need to ensure that they all happen within the scope of one session. Try not to call multiple DAO methods when each of them creates their own session and start and commit their own transactions. If you are being forced to do this, perhaps it's time to refactor.

Stateless session

There is another type of session that is supported by Hibernate, and this is stateless session. The reason this is called stateless is because there is no persistence context and all entities are considered detached. Additionally, there is the following:

- No automatic dirty checking. This means that you have to call `session. update()` before closing the session; otherwise, no update statement will be executed.

- No delayed DML (also known as write-behind). Every save or update will be executed right away. (Refer to the earlier discussion on action queues.)

- No cascade operation. You have to handle the associated entities.

- No proxy object; hence, no lazy fetching.

- No event notification or interceptors.

You should think of stateless sessions as direct calls to JDBC because this is essentially what occurs behind the scenes.

One good reason to use stateless sessions is to perform bulk operations. The memory footprint will be far less and, in some cases, it performs better.

Entity

A Hibernate entity is, typically, a sophisticated **Plain Old Java Object (POJO)**. It is sophisticated because it represents a business model whose data is assumed to be persistent. It's always decorated with various annotations, which enable additional characteristics, among other things. Or, it is configured using an hbm Hibernate mapping XML file. When an entity contains other entities, or a collection of other entities, this implies a database association for which you have to declare the proper mapping configuration to define the relationship type.

An entity can also embed other POJOs that are not entities. In such cases, the other entities are considered value objects. They have no identity, and have little business significance on their own. (We will discuss this further when we talk about the @Embedded and @Embeddable annotations in *Chapter 2, Advanced Mapping*).

Entity lifecycle

You should already be familiar with entity lifecycle. However, here is a different perspective of the different phases of the lifecycle.

Before discussing the lifecycle of an entity, it is important to not think of an entity as a POJO. Instead, if you keep reminding yourself that an entity is the persistent model of business data, you will easily understand the lifecycle.

The lifecycle begins when you instantiate an entity class. At this point, the entity has no presence in the persistence context; therefore, no data has been inserted in the database and no unique ID is assigned to the new entity. At this phase of the lifecycle, the entity is said to be in the *Transient* state.

Once you save your new entity by calling session.save(), your entity is now in the *Persistent* state, because at this point the session is managing it.

What happens to the entities after the session is closed? In this case, your entity has no presence in the persistence context, but it has a presence in the database. This state is called *Detached*.

There is another state, which is rarely mentioned, and this is the *Deleted* state. When you call `session.delete()` on an entity, it will fire off a `Delete` event and internally sets the entity state to `DELETED`. As long as the session is open, you can still undelete the entity by calling `session.persist()`.

There are certain lifecycle events that change the entity state, and those are well documented.

Types of entities

As mentioned earlier, you can declare a POJO class as your persistent class. There is another type of entity in Hibernate that is rarely used and perhaps not widely known, and this is map. This is known as a dynamic entity. You can use any implementation of the `java.util.Map` interface as a Hibernate entity. This is useful to implement a dynamic business model, which is great for the creation of a quick prototype. Ultimately, you are best off with POJO entities. If you need to implement a dynamic entity, first you can set the default entity mode to `MAP`:

```
Configuration configuration = new Configuration()
.configure()
.setProperty(Environment.DEFAULT_ENTITY_MODE,
EntityMode.MAP.toString());
```

Then, add a new mapping configuration. Hibernate uses the property name as a map key to get the value, for example, `<property name="firstname" .../>`. So, if your map contains other properties which are not included in the named map, they will be ignored by Hibernate:

```
<hibernate-mapping>
  <class entity-name="DynamicEntity">
    <id name="id" type="long" column="MAP_ID">
      <generator class="sequence" />
    </id>
    <property name="firstname" type="string" column="FIRSTNAME" />
    <property name="lastname" type="string" column="LASTNAME" />
  </class>
</hibernate-mapping>
```

Make sure that you add the new map to your Hibernate configuration. Now, you can use this as an entity. Note that when you call `session.save()`, you are passing the name of the entity as the first argument:

```
Map<String, String> myMap = new HashMap<String, String>();
myMap.put("firstname", "John");
myMap.put("lastname", "Smith");
```

```
 Session session = HibernateUtil
.getSessionFactory()
.getCurrentSession();
 Transaction transaction = session.beginTransaction();

 try {
    session.save("DynamicEntity", myMap); // notice entity name
    transaction.commit();
 }
catch (Exception e) {
    transaction.rollback();
    // log error
 }
 finally {
    if (session.isOpen())
      session.close();
 }
```

This used to be different in version 3.6. You didn't need to set the default entity mode on the configuration. The Session interface provided an API, which would return another session that supported dynamic entity. This was session.getSession(EntityMode.MAP), and this returned a new session, which inherited the JDBC connection and the transaction. However, this was removed in Hibernate 4.

Identity crisis

Each entity class has a property that is marked as the unique identifier of that entity. This could be a primitive data type or another Java class, which would represent a composite ID. (You'll see this in *Chapter 2*, *Advanced Mapping*, when we talk about mapping) For now, having an ID is still optional, but in future releases of Hibernate, this will no longer be the case and every entity class must have an ID attribute.

Furthermore, as Hibernate is responsible for generating and setting the ID, you should always protect it by making sure that the setter method for the ID is private so that you don't accidentally set the ID in your code. Hibernate can access private fields using reflection. Hibernate also requires entities to have a no-arg constructor.

In some cases, you have to override the `equals()` and `hashCode()` methods, especially if you are keeping the detached objects around and want to reattach them or need to add them to a set. This is because outside of the persistence context the Java equality may fail even though you are comparing two entity instances that represent the same row. The default implementation of the `equals()` method only checks whether the two instances are the same reference.

If you are sure that both objects have an ID assigned, then, in addition to reference equality check, you can compare their identifiers for equality. If you can't rely on the ID property but an entity can be uniquely identified by a business key, such as user ID or social security number, then you can compare the business keys.

It's not a good idea to compare all properties for equality check. There are several reasons, as follows:

- First, if you keep a detached object around and then retrieve it again in another session, Hibernate can't tell that they are the same entities if you modify one of them.

- Second, you may have a long list of properties and your code will look messy, and if you add a new property, you may forget to modify the `equals()` method.

- Finally, this approach will lead to equal entities if you have multiple database rows with the same values, and they should be treated as different entities because they represent different rows. (For example, if two people live at the same address and one person moves, you may accidentally change the address for both.)

Beyond JPA

When you decorate your class with annotations, you are empowering your objects with additional features. There are certain features that are provided by Hibernate, which are not available in JPA.

Most of these features are provided through Hibernate annotations, which are packaged separately. Some annotations affect the behavior of your entity, and some are there to make mapping easier and more powerful.

The behavior modifying annotations that are worth noting here are as follows:

- `@Immutable`: This makes an entity immutable.

- `@SelectBeforeUpdate`: This is great for reducing unnecessary updates to the database and reducing contention. However, it does make an extra call through JDBC.

- **@BatchSize**: This can be used to limit the size of a collection on fetch.

- **@DynamicInsert** and **@DynamicUpdat**: These prevent null properties from being included in the dynamic SQL generation for both insert and update.

- **@OptimisticLocking**: This is used to define the type of optimistic lock.

- **@Fetch**: This can be used to define **@FetchMode**. You can instruct Hibernate to use Join, Select, or Sub Select. The Join query uses outer join to load the related entities, the Select query issues individual SQL select statements, and Sub Select is self-explanatory. (This is different from JPA's **@FetchType**, which is used to decide to perform lazy fetch or not.)

- **@Filter**: This is used to limit the entities that are returned.

It's worth exploring both the org.hibernate.annotations JavaDocs and the JPA annotations. We will cover Hibernate annotations (beyond JPA) that modify mappings and associations in the next chapter, when we discuss mappings. We will also return to @Fetch and @Filter when we discuss Fetching in *Chapter 4, Advanced Fetching*.

Proxy objects

If you are familiar with Java reflection, you have heard of the java.lang.reflect. Proxy class. In a nutshell, you can wrap any object with a proxy and intercept calls to methods of that object using an invocation handler. Many Java frameworks use proxy objects, or manipulate bytecode (also called instrumentation) to modify the behavior of an object. Hibernate uses both ways for different purposes. More importantly, Hibernate implements its own set of wrapper classes for collection types. (Refer to classes in org.hibernate.collection.internal.)

If you fetch an entity, Hibernate doesn't fetch the associated collections if they are marked as lazy fetch. Instead, it waits until you actually try to access the associated collection. As soon as you access an entity in the associated collection, Hibernate will fetch the associated entities from the persistence store and will then populate the wrapped collection for you to access. Hibernate accomplishes this using the internal collection wrappers. You can actually examine this yourself by writing a simple check, as follows:

```
parent = (Parent) session.get(Parent.class, new Long(1));
Set<Child> children = parent.getChildren();
if (children instanceof PersistentSet) {
  System.out.println("**** Not java.util.Set");
}

// PersistentSet is located in org.hibernate.collection.internal
```

Hibernate uses byte code manipulation techniques to initialize an object that is uninitialized. This usually occurs when your entity has an associated entity, for example, a `Person` entity that is associated with an `Address` entity. When the `root` entity, in this case `Person`, is loaded from the database, the `Address` object is not initialized in case of `LAZY` loading. In such cases, Hibernate returns a manipulated version of the associated entity, and as soon as you try to access any of the attributes of the associated entity, for example, `address.getStreet()`, Hibernate will hit the database to `fetch` the values for the associated entity and initialize it.

Hibernate also returns a proxy object when you ask for an entity using the `load` method instead of the `get` method of the `Session` class.

 The byte code manipulation is achieved using the `Javassist` library.

When working with Hibernate, it is important that you keep in mind how Hibernate uses proxy objects.

Batch processing

When you interact with the session by saving entities or fetching them from the DB, Hibernate keeps them around in the persistent context until the session is closed, or until you evict the object or clear the session. This is Hibernate's first-level cache.

Care must be taken when executing queries that load many objects or when trying to save a large set of entities. If you don't perform some cleanup work, your JVM will run out of memory in the middle of the work unit.

There are certain things you can do to avoid such situations. Some of them are manual work, and others are managed by Hibernate if you provide enough hints or if you use the right session type.

 How does Hibernate know whether it should call JDBC `executeBatch`? This decision is made in the entity persister, which is responsible for persisting an entity via JDBC. Hibernate keeps track of all the DML statements for each entity type, and when the statement count is more than 1 for a particular entity type, it will use batch execution.

Manual batch management

One way to ensure that batch processing is under control is by manually managing the population of the first-level cache, that is, the persistent context. If you are saving or updating a batch of entities, you can occasionally flush and clear the session. Flushing the session will execute all the pending SQL statements, and when you clear the session, all the entities are evicted from the persistent context.

You can do this by forcing a flush and clear, as follows:

```java
public void saveStudents(List<Map<String, String>> students) {
  final int batchSize = 15;
  Session session = HibernateUtil
.getSessionFactory()
.getCurrentSession();
  Transaction transaction = session.beginTransaction();
  try {
    int i = 0;
    for (Map<String, String> studentMap:students) {
      i++;
      Student student = new Student();
      student.setFirstname(studentMap.get("firstname"));
      student.setLastname(studentMap.get("lastname"));
      session.save(student);

      if (i % batchSize == 0) {
        session.flush();
        session.clear();
      }
    }
    transaction.commit();
  }
  catch (Exception e) {
    transaction.rollback();
    // log stack trace
  }
  finally {
    if (session.isOpen())
      session.close();
  }
}
```

You should use the same mechanism when you are fetching entities. There is a slight performance hit when you flush and clear the session. However, this is not significant. Your JDBC connection is still open, and the transaction is still active, and these are the expensive resources whose lifecycle you need to be concerned with in your design. (Refer to the earlier discussion on contextual session.)

Setting batch size

When you flush the session, you are essentially submitting the appropriate SQL statements to the JDBC layer. In the JDBC world, you can either execute a single statement, or you can batch statements and when ready, execute the batch (refer to the `java.sql.Statement.addBatch(...)` and `executeBatch()` methods).

There is no batch size in JDBC, but Hibernate uses the property called `jdbc.batch_size` to control how many entities will be in a batch. This doesn't mean that if you set this, you don't have to worry about memory exhaustion; you still have to manually manage the persistent context for a large sized batch. This just means that when Hibernate determines that it can batch DML statements, how many times does it call `addBatch(...)` before calling `executeBatch()`.

There is another batch size setting, which comes in the form of annotation, and this is `@BatchSize`, which is used to decorate an entity class. This setting is not for batch inserts or updates; this is used at fetch time for collections and entities when they are loaded lazily.

Using stateless session

Stateless session was introduced earlier. As there is no persistent context in a stateless session, you don't need to flush or clear the session. All the changes to your entities are reflected immediately in the database as there is no delayed write. Remember, there is no cascade operation on associated entities, and the associated collections are ignored. So, you have to manually manage all the entities.

Summary

The purpose of this chapter was to expose the internals of Hibernate as they relate to session and entity. This should help you understand Hibernate better, design and write more elegant code, and when you encounter errors, understand the error messages clearly.

You will see a lot more sample code in later chapters, but in this chapter, we focused more on understanding Hibernate, and less on samples.

We learned about session and its behavior in various contexts. We also learned about entity, explored its lifecycle, and also learned about map types, which is a dynamic entity. Furthermore, the discussion on entity identity is very important and deserves careful attention. As discussed in this chapter, Hibernate offers a rich set of features, which are not available in JPA. We will see more of them in future chapters. Finally, we talked about proxy objects and batch processing.

This chapter is the heaviest in content. In the following chapters, we will focus on specific topics and explore different ways to accomplish certain objectives using Hibernate. The next chapter covers mapping concepts, and you will take a look at how basic and advanced mapping can fill the gap between objects and relations.

2
Advanced Mapping

In this chapter, we will explore mapping concepts. This is at the core of the Object-Relational Mapping challenge to correctly map Java objects and classes to their persistence representation. As discussed in the previous chapter, the object-oriented world has a lot in common with the relational world, attributes, types, and so on. The ORM solutions, such as Hibernate, were created to address their notable differences, inheritance, composition, object reference and identification, and much more. After reading this chapter, you will be able to correctly map database identification to a class attribute using primitive data types or a more complex Java class. You will also see how to create associations between objects and annotate them correctly so that Hibernate has enough information about the relationships between table data. Furthermore, you will be able to instruct Hibernate to perform cascaded operations and map classes as part of an inheritance model. Finally, you will see how to work with enumerated types and create your own custom type.

In this chapter, we will cover the following topics:

- Mapping concepts:
    - Instance and row
    - Annotation verses XML
    - Owning entity
    - Value mapping
    - JPA ID generation
    - Hibernate ID generation
    - Composite ID

- Association cardinality:
  - One-to-one association
  - One-to-many association
  - Many-to-many association
  - Self-referencing tables
- Cascade operations
- Inheritance:
  - Single table strategy
  - Table per class strategy
  - Joined strategy
- Custom mapped data type

Mapping concepts

Mapping objects to relations is the core mission of Hibernate, and as we discussed previously, this can be a difficult challenge that can only be overcome by understanding the fundamental concepts.

Let's explore mapping concepts by reviewing some of the fundamentals of relational databases, such as relational algebra, simple and composite IDs, join tables, and foreign keys.

Instances and rows

The origin of relational database concepts is *Relational Algebra*, which is based on *Set Theory*. Just as we think of objects as instances of classes, you should also think of a database row (a tuple) as an element of a set (the relation) that is defined by the database tab.

For example, if your object graph contains an instance of the Person entity class that represents John and another instance that represents Sara, you should think of these as two rows in the Person table.

In both cases, by being an instance of a class or a row of a table, they agree to possess certain attributes, such as identification, first name, and last name:

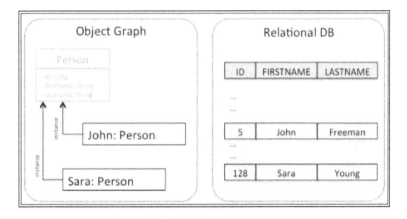

Obviously, in real-life scenarios, we always have more than one table, which are almost always associated with each other, whose corresponding object graph has a hierarchy of objects that belong to the same or different classes. For example, in the following figure, the instance of the Person class with id: 2 is the *owner* of two other instances of the same class; Alex is the parent of both John and Sara. It also co-owns the "m" address instance whose other owner is the John instance, indicating that Alex and John both live at the same house and Sara lives at a different location. The following figure shows how an object graph compares with a relational model:

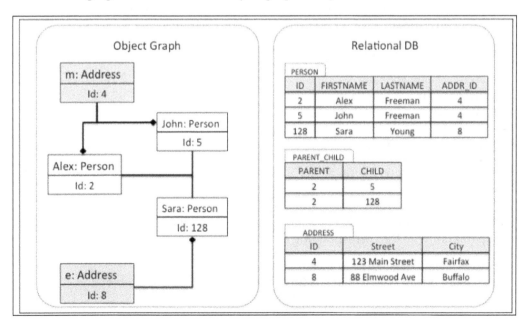

In this example, we see an additional table that defines the association between a parent and a child. The PARENT_CHILD table only defines the hierarchal association and on its own doesn't have any significance. This is called a join table or an association table. This table doesn't represent an entity, and it only exists to define the association between the entities. This association is declared in Java, using an annotation or a mapping configuration.

You may have noticed that the PERSON and PARENT_CHILD tables seem unnecessarily normalized; that is, you can simply add a PARENT column to the PERSON table to create a self-referencing table, which will perform the same trick. (You'll see a mapping example of self-referencing tables later in this chapter). This is simply a design decision and the correct design depends on the situation. For example, if the entity in the object graph can have more than one parent, for example, in case of associating a father and mother, or with many students having many teachers, a join table is clearly a better solution and sometimes unavoidable. In other cases where you may only have a small percentage of data tuples in your set that are associated with other tuples of the same set, using a self-referencing table will leave holes in the underlying data structure. (Many rows will have a NULL value for the PARENT column.) Use your best judgment.

Annotation versus XML

In Hibernate, any Plain Ole Java Object (POJO) can be treated as an entity. However, you still have to provide a mapping configuration between the class attributes or methods and database columns and rows. This configuration is done using an annotation or a Hibernate mapping XML file, hbm.xml.

Consider an Address entity:

```
public class Address {
    private int id;
    private String street;
    private String city;
    private String state;
    private String zipCode;
    // getters and setters
}
```

The following shows a sample Hibernate mapping XML file, called Address.hbm.xml, to map this entity to the corresponding database relation:

```
<hibernate-mapping>
  <class name="com.packt.hibernate.ch2.listing01.Address"
    table="ADDRESS">
```

```
    <id name="id" type="int" column="id">
      <generator class="native" />
    </id>
    <property name="street" column="STREET" type="string"/>
    <property name="city" column="CITY" type="string"/>
    <property name="state" column="STATE" type="string"/>
    <property name="zipCode" column="ZIP_CODE"
    type="string"/>
  </class>
</hibernate-mapping>
```

You need to add the `Address.hbm.xml` file to the main Hibernate configuration, and as long as the XML file is located in the class path, for example, in the resources directory, then Hibernate can find it:

```
<hibernate-configuration>
  <session-factory>
    <property name="connection.driver_class">
      org.postgresql.Driver
    </property>
    <property …/>
    <property …/>
    <mapping resource="Address.hbm.xml"/>
  </session-factory>
</hibernate-configuration>
```

Alternatively, you can use an annotation to create this mapping. Consider the following entity:

```
@Entity
public class Person {
  @Id
  @GeneratedValue
  private long id;
  private String firstname;
  private String lastname;
  private String ssn;
  private Date birthdate;

  @ManyToOne
  private Address address;
  // getters and setters
}
```

As using an annotation is the preferred method for developers, we will mainly use annotations throughout this book.

Owning entity

When you read through JPA or Hibernate JavaDocs, you may come across the term *owning entity*. It is important to understand this when you deal with the various types of associations (one-to-one, one-to-many, and so on) as well as Cascade operations. One way to think about an owning entity, in an association, is to think about the entity that directly knows of all the other entities in any association. For example, in the object graph earlier, the Object with ID 2 (Alex) is clearly the owning entity of the other person instances because it knows about Object ID 5 (John) and 128 (Sara), but the children don't know about each other without going through the parent. Furthermore, in the person-address association, the person instance is the owning entity as the address by itself is meaningless.

Another way to interpret an owning entity is by the directionality of the association. If an entity A is fully informed of an association, for example, by having a reference to another entity B, and B has no knowledge of the association, then their association is *unidirectional* and A is the owning entity.

The definition of an owning entity is even more evident when we discuss value objects, which we'll do in the next section.

Value mapping

Not every Java object that is persisted or fetched has to be declared as an Entity. You may have a class that represents an encapsulation of a set of data (values) that independently doesn't have any significance. However, if you associate this with an entity that can be referenced by an ID, then it becomes significant. This is known as a value type.

Value types have the following properties:

- They do *not* have an ID
- They shall not be shared between entities
- They cannot be stored independently of the owning entity
- They may be stored in a separate table
- They can be used as a composite ID for an entity

A good example of a value type is the address data, house, street, city, state, and so on. You can create a class called Address with these properties and use the Address type as a property in your entity class. Another good example is metrics and analytics—for instance GPS coordinates or daily statistics, such as the opening and closing price, the day's high and low, volume, and so on.

You do have to carefully decide what should be treated as a value type in your design as it depends on the business domain. For example, in a problem domain where people are customers and goods are items being sold, it's very likely that address can be treated as a value type. However, in a different domain, for example a real estate search engine, the address is most likely the most important Entity in the database.

You can use the @Embeddable annotation to declare a value type, and then, in your entity, when you use the value type to declare a property, you can use the @Embedded annotation. If you don't use annotation, use the <component/> tag in your mapping configuration.

Consider the following example, where DailyStats is declared as a value type. Note that this class has no ID:

```
@Embeddable
public class DailyStats {
   private double openingPrice;
   private double closingPrice;
   private double high;
   private double low;
   private long volume;

   // getters and setters
}
```

This is then used as a type to declare a property in another class:

```
@Entity
public class DailyStockPrice {

   @Id
   @GeneratedValue(strategy = GenerationType.AUTO)
   private long id;
   private Date date;

   @Embedded
   private DailyStats dailyStats;

   // getters and setters

   public DailyStats getDailyStats() {
      if (dailyStats == null) {
       return null;
```

```
        }

        DailyStats copy = new DailyStats();
        copy.setOpeningPrice(dailyStats.getOpeningPrice());
        copy.setClosingPrice(dailyStats.getClosingPrice());
        copy.setHigh(dailyStats.getHigh());
        copy.setLow(dailyStats.getLow());
        copy.setVolume(dailyStats.getVolume());

        return copy;
    }
}
```

As you can see, the getter and setter methods are not shown here, except one: `getDailyStats()`. This method doesn't return the instance that is owned by this entity, it returns a copy. This is to ensure that the value type is not accidentally shared between entities.

If you wish to store the value type in its own table, you can do this by declaring a secondary table and overriding the attributes of the embedded value type to reference the columns of the secondary table, as shown here:

```
@Entity
@SecondaryTable(
    name = "daily_stats",
    pkJoinColumns = {
      @PrimaryKeyJoinColumn(name="id")
    })
public class DailyStockPrice {

  @Id
  @GeneratedValue(strategy = GenerationType.AUTO)
  private long id;
  private Date date;

  @Embedded
  @AttributeOverrides({
    @AttributeOverride(name="openingPrice",
      column=@Column(name="openingPrice", table="daily_stats")),
    @AttributeOverride(name="closingPrice",
      column=@Column(name="closingPrice", table="daily_stats")),
    @AttributeOverride(name="high",
```

```
        column=@Column(name="high", table="daily_stats")),
    @AttributeOverride(name="low",
      column=@Column(name="low", table="daily_stats")),
    @AttributeOverride(name="volume",
      column=@Column(name="volume", table="daily_stats"))
  })
  private DailyStats dailyStats;

  // getters and setters
}
```

This will cause Hibernate to perform a left outer join operation between the primary and the secondary table when it fetches an entity that has a secondary table. (You can also use this trick to force Hibernate to perform arbitrary joins between tables.)

Later in this chapter, we will see how to use value types as composite keys for an entity when we discuss ID generation.

JPA ID generation

As mentioned in the previous chapter, all entities require an identifier. There are two main concepts to consider when dealing with entity identifiers: the **structure** and **generator** strategies.

Most of the time, your table has a single primary key column that can simply be mapped to a class field or property of any primitive type, as well as the String and date types. If the primary key is defined by more than one column, you need to use a composite ID structure, which is discussed in a later section.

When your table has a single column as the primary key, simply use the @Id annotation and tell Hibernate which strategy to use to generate identifiers.

 Keep in mind that, when you save a new entity, you may not have an identifier until after the flush is completed.

In the JPA world, there are only four types of generation strategy: AUTO, IDENTITY, SEQUENCE, and TABLE. All of these are well explained in the JPA JavaDoc, except the TABLE strategy, which might require a bit of an explanation.

The TABLE generation strategy is used in conjunction with the @TableGenerator annotation. You can allocate a table in your schema to hold all of your sequences and then instruct JPA (in this case, Hibernate) to use this table. Consider the following classes:

```
@Entity
public class Player {

  @Id
  @TableGenerator(name = "TABLE_GENERATOR",
    table = "ALL_SEQUENCES",
    pkColumnName = "TABLE_NAME",
    valueColumnName = "NEXT_ID",
    allocationSize=1)
  @GeneratedValue(strategy = GenerationType.TABLE,
    generator = "TABLE_GENERATOR")
  private long id;
  private String name;

  // getters and setters
}

@Entity
public class Game {

  @Id
  @TableGenerator(name = "TABLE_GENERATOR",
    table = "ALL_SEQUENCES",
    pkColumnName = "TABLE_NAME",
    valueColumnName = "NEXT_ID",
    allocationSize=1)
  @GeneratedValue(strategy = GenerationType.TABLE,
    generator = "TABLE_GENERATOR")
  private long id;
  private String name;

  // getters and setters
}
```

They both use the same generator, defined by the @TableGenerator annotation, which points to the same sequence table, called ALL_SEQUENCES. After you insert two new players (in the Player table) and three new games (in the Game table), this is what ALL_SEQUENCES table will look like:

TABLE_NAME	NEXT_ID
Player	3
Game	4

Clearly, additional SQL will be executed when you use the table generation strategy. This has little performance impact if you are not inserting new entities at a high volume; otherwise, you should be mindful of this in cases where a large number of entities are being inserted.

Hibernate ID generation

Hibernate provides additional strategies to generate values for ID columns. Each one has a special feature that can be used to solve specific problems. To use the strategies that are provided by Hibernate, first you need to create a custom generator using the @GenericGenerator annotation in Hibernate and then, in the @GeneratedValue, refer to your custom generator:

```
@Entity
@org.hibernate.annotations.GenericGenerator (
    name= "custom-generator",
    strategy="sequence"
)
public class ShoppingCart {

  @Id
  @GeneratedValue(generator="custom-generator")
  private long id;
  private Date createdTime;

  // getters and setters
}
```

The generator strategies that are only available in Hibernate are increment, hilo, seqhilo, uuid, uuid2, guid, native, assigned, select, foreign, and sequence-identity. We will only discuss the UUID and foreign generation strategy.

The UUID strategy implements the specifications in RFC 4122. This is an ID that is presumably unique universally. However, in reality this is only unique within a domain and it is designed so that unique ID generation is not a central task and can be accomplished by any node in a distributed environment.

Another very useful strategy is the use of foreign keys. In a one-to-one association, the entities are tightly connected and it makes sense to pick the same identification for both ends of the association. The code here shows an example of how to achieve this:

```
@Entity
public class Circle {

    @Id
    @GeneratedValue
    private long id;
    private float radius;
    @OneToOne
    @PrimaryKeyJoinColumn
    private Center center;

    // getters and setters
}

@Entity
@org.hibernate.annotations.GenericGenerator(name = "custom-generator",
strategy = "foreign", parameters = { @Parameter(name = "property",
value = "circle") })
public class Center {

    @Id
    @GeneratedValue(generator = "custom-generator")
    private long id;
    private float xPos;
    private float yPos;

    @OneToOne
    @PrimaryKeyJoinColumn
    private Circle circle;

    // getters and setters

}
```

We will discuss the `@OneToOne` association later in this chapter. There is actually an easy way to accomplish the foreign key strategy in JPA:

```
@Entity
public class Car implements Serializable{

  @Id
  @GeneratedValue(strategy = GenerationType.AUTO)
  private long id;
  private String model;

// getters and setters
}

@Entity
public class Engine implements Serializable {
  @Id @OneToOne
  @JoinColumn(name = "car_id")
  private Car car;
  private long size;

  // getters and setters
}
```

Composite ID

In cases where more than one attribute is required to uniquely identify an entity, you'll need to use a composite ID. Hibernate allows you to annotate multiple properties with the `@Id` annotation to create a composite ID. JPA requires the use of a component (embeddable) and the `@EmbeddedId` annotation. You must always implement `equals` and `hashCode` for composite IDs (refer to the identity discussion in the previous chapter):

```
@Embeddable
public class RoomId implements Serializable {
  private long roomNumber;
  private long buildingNumber;

  // getters and setters

  @Override
  public int hashCode() {
    final int prime = 31;
    int result = 1;
```

```java
    result = prime * result
    + (int) (buildingNumber ^ (buildingNumber >>> 32));
    result = prime * result + (int) (roomNumber ^ (roomNumber >>>
    32));
    return result;
  }

  @Override
  public boolean equals(Object obj) {
    if (this == obj)
    return true;
    if (obj == null)
      return false;
    if (getClass() != obj.getClass())
      return false;
    RoomId other = (RoomId) obj;
    if (buildingNumber != other.buildingNumber)
    return false;
    if (roomNumber != other.roomNumber)
      return false;
    return true;
  }

}

@Entity
public class Room implements Serializable {

  @EmbeddedId
  private RoomId id;
  private double length;
  private double width;

  // getters and setters

}
```

As mentioned earlier, with Hibernate, you don't have to use an embedded ID. You can simply annotate the fields that you would like to include in your composite ID. You still have to implement `equals` and `hashCode`:

```java
@Entity
public class Room implements Serializable {

  @Id private long roomNumber;
```

```
@Id private long buildingNumber;
private double length;
private double width;

// getters and setters
// don't forget equals and hashCode
}
```

Later, you'll see how to create a more complex composite ID for an entity that is associated with another entity whose ID is also used in the composition.

Association cardinality

Just as relational databases define the cardinality of table relationships, ORM solutions also define the cardinality of entity associations. Before we discuss how to map associations, let's review how associations are created in a relational database. The following are the two types of relationship:

- **Foreign key relationship:** You can relate a table to another by declaring a column as a foreign key of the other table. This is typically used for a 1:1 (one-to-one) or a M:1 (many-to-one) relationship. If you make the foreign key column UNIQUE, then you are defining a 1:1 relationship; otherwise, this is M:1. If you make it NULLABLE, then the relationship is optional; that is, 1:0, 1:1, M:0, or M:1.

- **Join table relationship:** Another way to relate two tables is by creating a join table that will have at least two columns that store the primary keys of the rows that should be related. This is typically used for 1:M and M:N relationships. Both columns should be NON-NULLABLE.

One-to-one associations

Typically, in a relational database, when we refer to a one-to-one (1:1) relationship, we are really talking about one-to-zero (1:0) and one-to-one (1:1). This is because, to define a tight one-to-one relationship between OCCUPANT and ROOM, for example, we have to declare a foreign key from the OCCUPANT table to the ROOM table, and another foreign key from ROOM back to OCCUPANT table. There are two issues with this:

- When inserting or deleting data, you have to defer integrity constraints and this complicates matters

- Such a tight relationship indicates that two tables should really be one because one cannot exist without the other

This is why, in reality, a one-to-one association is really a `one-to-zero_or_one`. In this case, we identify an entity as the **owning entity**. For example, ROOM can exist without an OCCUPANT; hence, ROOM is the rightful owner of the relationship.

Another thing to keep in mind is the notion of *direction*. An association can be **unidirectional** or **bidirectional**. This simply defines a connection between two entities so that we can get to one from the other. If both can be reached either way, then it's a bidirectional relationship. Clearly, the notion of direction doesn't make sense in a relational database. If you can join two tables on a common column, then they are connected, but there is no such thing as direction, which implies reachability.

In a unidirectional association, if the referenced entity table has a foreign key constraint back to the owning entity table, you should use the `@PrimaryKeyJoinColumn` annotation on the referenced entity attribute. Let's revisit the ROOM example, this time adding the following occupant:

```
@Entity
public class Occupant {
  @Id
  private RoomId roomId;
  private Date checkinDate;
  private Date checkoutDate;
  // getters and setters
}

@Entity
public class Room {
  @Id
  private RoomId id;
  private double length;
  private double width;

  @OneToOne(cascade=CascadeType.ALL)
  @PrimaryKeyJoinColumn
  private Occupant occupant;
  // getters and setters
}
```

As you can see, it doesn't matter whether the ID of the owning entity is a simple or a composite ID. Ultimately, each ID column becomes a key in the secondary table.

In order to create a bidirectional association, both entities must have a reference to each other. To demonstrate this, let's rewrite the Car and Engine entities, as shown here (note that Engine no longer shares its ID with Car, as it did earlier.):

```
@Entity
public class Car {

    @Id
    @GeneratedValue(strategy = GenerationType.AUTO)
    private long id;
    private String model;
    @OneToOne
    private Engine engine;
    // getters and setters
}

@Entity
public class Engine {
    @Id
    @GeneratedValue(strategy = GenerationType.AUTO)
    private long id;
    @OneToOne
    private Car car;
    private long size;
    // getters and setters
}
```

In this case, there is a tight association between the two entities. In fact, if you use Hibernate to generate the DDL for you, it will create two-way foreign key constraints, which we discussed earlier, and this might be problematic. Luckily, Hibernate creates a nullable foreign key, and it can insert the Car entity first with a NULL engine ID as it doesn't know the engine ID yet, then inserts the Engine entity, which now has an identifier. Finally, it updates the Car row to set the foreign key to the engine ID.

When persisting both Car and Engine, you need to make the association in Java; otherwise, Hibernate will not populate the foreign key columns:

```
Car car = new Car();
car.setModel("toyota");
Engine engine = new Engine();
engine.setSize(1500);
engine.setCar(car);
car.setEngine(engine);
```

```
Session session = HibernateUtil
.getSessionFactory()
.getCurrentSession();
Transaction transaction = session.beginTransaction();
try {
session.save(car);
session.save(engine);

transaction.commit();
}
catch (Exception e) {
transaction.rollback();
// log stack trace
}
finally {
if (session.isOpen())
session.close();
}
```

In the next section, we will explore how to work with one-to-many associations.

One-to-many associations

When dealing with associations of the many nature, it's best if you think of the ownership of the association. Earlier, we defined ownership as the entity that knows of the other end of the association and is able to reach the associated entity. A hotel room can know a list of its occupants, but an occupant may not know to which room it belongs without exploring all rooms. In this case, the Room entity is the owner of the association.

Let's use the ROOM and OCCUPANT example to explain this.

If you create a one-to-many association between the Room and Occupant entities, Hibernate likes to create a join table in the database to keep track of this association. In this case, the Room entity keeps track of Occupants in a collection and Occupant has a simple ID:

```
@Entity
public class Room {
  @Id
  private RoomId id;
  private double length;
  private double width;
  @OneToMany(cascade=CascadeType.ALL)
```

```
    private Collection<Occupant> occupants;
    // getters and setters
}

@Entity
public class Occupant {
  @Id
  @GeneratedValue
  private long id;
  private Date checkinDate;
  private Date checkoutDate;
  // getters and setters
}
```

This will only work if there is a join table between the ROOM table and the OCCUPANT tables (keep in mind that ROOM has a composite primary key, building number, and room number):

ROOM:			
buildingnumber	**roomnumber**	**length**	**width**
4	5	8.5	12.4

OCCUPANT:		
id	**checkindate**	**checkoutdate**
1	1/1/2015	1/3/2015
2	1/3/2015	1/6/2015

ROOM_OCCUPANT:		
room_buildingnumber	**room_roomnumber**	**occupants_id**
4	5	1
4	5	2

If you'd like to eliminate the join table, you can add a reference to the room ID in the Occupant entity and set the mappedBy attribute in the @OneToMany annotation:

```
@Entity
public class Room {
  @Id
  private RoomId id;
  private double length;
```

```
    private double width;

    @OneToMany(cascade=CascadeType.ALL, mappedBy="roomId")
    private Collection<Occupant> occupants;
    // getters and setters
}

@Entity
public class Occupant {
    @Id
    @GeneratedValue
    private long id;
    private RoomId roomId;
    private Date checkinDate;
    private Date checkoutDate;
}
```

This will eliminate the need for a join table, but it adds additional columns to the OCCUPANT table to associate each record with the appropriate room. In this case, the primary key of the owner entity (Room) is stored as foreign key in the owned entity (Occupant):

PERSON					
DTYPE	ID	FIRSTNAME	LASTNAME	DEST	LIC_NUM
Person	1	Steve	Jones		
Driver	2	John	Cooper		52-23455221
Passenger	3	Sara	Davis	NYC	

Many-to-one associations

If you reverse the ownership of the association, then you will have a many-to-one relationship from Occupant to Room. This time, Hibernate can't get a list of the occupants for you, when you fetch a Room entity. You'll have to look up the occupants by room ID using an additional query. However, if you make the association bidirectional, that is, both entities know of each other, you can get to one from the other without any additional work.

Additionally, Hibernate provides a @NotFound annotation that is quite useful in the case of a many-to-one relationship. Use this annotation for cases where the other end of the association doesn't exist, perhaps because there are no integrity constraints. The default action is to throw an exception, but you can also set it to ignore. (Note that this is not available in JPA.)

Many-to-many associations

When entities should have a many-to-many association, you can let Hibernate know this using the @ManyToMany annotation. If you just add the @ManyToMany annotation to both sides of the association, Hibernate will create two join tables, one for each "owning entity." We saw similar behavior earlier with the one-to-many association. To eliminate the extra join table, we can use the same trick, that is, we use the mappedBy attribute of the @ManyToMany annotation. You can't add this to both sides. The mappedBy attribute is used on the "owned" entity, that is, if you consider teacher to be the owner of students, then add mappedBy to @ManyToMany of the Student entity:

```
@Entity
public class Teacher {
  ...
  @ManyToMany
  private Collection<Student> students;
  ...
}

@Entity
public class Student {
  ...
  @ManyToMany(mappedBy="students")
  private Collection<Teacher> teachers;
  ...
}
```

Self-referencing tables

You can think of a self-referencing table as an entity that has a one-to-many and a many-to-one association with itself. Based on our discussion on these topics, it should be easy to write the mapping for a self-referencing table, as follows:

```
@Entity
public class Node {

  @Id
  @GeneratedValue
  private long id;
  private String name;

  @ManyToOne(cascade=CascadeType.ALL)
  private Node parent;
```

```
@OneToMany(mappedBy="parent")
private Collection<Node> children = new ArrayList<Node>();
// getters and setters
}
```

When you persist the entities, make sure that the associations are created on both sides; that is, add the children to the parent and set the parent for each child:

```
Node parent = new Node();
parent.setName("parent1");

Node child1 = new Node();
child1.setName("child1");
child1.setParent(parent);

parent.getChildren().add(child1);

Node child2 = new Node();
child2.setName("child2");
child2.setParent(parent);

parent.getChildren().add(child2);

try {
  Session session = NodeHibernateUtil
    .getSessionFactory()
    .getCurrentSession();
  Transaction transaction = session.beginTransaction();
  try {
   session.save(parent);
   session.save(child1);
   session.save(child2);

   transaction.commit();
  }
  catch (Exception e) {
    transaction.rollback();
    // log stack trace
  }
  finally {
    if (session.isOpen())
      session.close();
  }
```

```
    }
    catch (Exception e) {
    e.printStackTrace();
}
```

If the entities that are mapped to a self-referencing table have a many-to-many association, you have to create a join table to accommodate this association.

Cascade operations

You may already be familiar with cascade delete and update in a relational database. In the ORM world, this notion is a little more complicated. Hibernate treats this as a transitive property that may or may not propagate to the associated entities, depending on the state of the objects (transient, detached, or persistent) as well as the cascade settings that you choose when you define your association.

Hibernate doesn't automatically propagate the persistence operations to the associated entities. However, you can control this behavior using the cascade attribute of an association.

JPA defines certain cascade types: ALL, DETACH, MERGE, PERSIST, REFRESH, and REMOVE. These correspond directly with the operations provided by the EntityManager interface.

The Hibernate Session interface provides additional operations, such as save, update, or replicate (some names are different in Hibernate and JPA but the underlying operations are the same; for example, detach versus evict, or remove versus delete.) Therefore, Hibernate defines additional cascade types that you can use.

One notable cascade type is DELETE_ORPHAN, which is used to delete entities that are no longer being referenced by a parent entity. This type has been deprecated and is now available in newer versions of JPA as metadata, called orphanRemoval, for the @OneToOne and @OneToMany annotations. This only works when you disassociate a one-to-one or when you remove the entity from a one-to-many collection.

Inheritance

One of the biggest challenges in mapping objects to relations is inheritance. Relational databases do not support this concept. So, ORM solutions need to get creative when dealing with this issue. JPA specifies several strategies, all of which are implemented by Hibernate and these will be discussed here.

Single table strategy

The default strategy to support class hierarchy, in the case of inheritance, is single table strategy. If you don't specify any strategy, Hibernate will look for (or create) a single table with the name of the parent class. This table has columns for every attribute in all the classes in the inheritance model. Let's consider the following superclass and its subclasses:

```
@Entity
public class Person {
  @Id
  @GeneratedValue
  private long id;

  private String firstname;
  private String lastname;

}

@Entity
public class Driver extends Person {

  @Column(name="LIC_NUM")
  private String licenseNumber;

}

@Entity
public class Passenger extends Person {

  @Column(name="DEST")
  private String destination;

}
```

Note that all the classes are annotated as entity and the children inherit the `id` property from the parent. If you enable Hibernate schema generation and save a `Person` entity, a `Driver` entity, and a `Passenger` entity, your table will look like the following:

PERSON					
DTYPE	ID	FIRSTNAME	LASTNAME	DEST	LIC_NUM
Person	1	Steve	Jones		
Driver	2	John	Cooper		52-23455221
Passenger	3	Sara	Davis	NYC	

The first thing to note is a column called DTYPE. This is a column that's created by Hibernate and is used to distinguish between the different rows. The value in this column tells Hibernate which class it maps to.

Also, note that the Person row doesn't have a value in the DEST and LIC_NUM column. That's because the Person class doesn't have an attribute with these names. On the other hand, the Driver entity has a license number, and Passenger has a destination.

You can apply further customization. For example, using @DiscriminatorColumn on the parent class, you can set the name of the Discriminator column:

```
@Entity
@DiscriminatorColumn(name="PERSON_TYPE")
public class Person {
  @Id
  @GeneratedValue
  private long id;

  private String firstname;
  private String lastname;
}
```

You can also instruct Hibernate to use a different value (and different type) for the discriminator column:

```
@Entity
@DiscriminatorColumn(name="PERSON_TYPE", discriminatorType=Discriminat
orType.INTEGER)
@DiscriminatorValue(value="100")
public class Person {
...
}

@Entity
@DiscriminatorValue(value="200")
public class Driver extends Person {
...
}

@Entity
@DiscriminatorValue(value="300")
public class Passenger extends Person {
...
}
```

> The single table strategy is not ideal, but it's simple and may be perfect for simple situations. However, this strategy might lead to a highly denormalized schema and leave a lot of holes in the table. Furthermore, in real life scenarios, a class will have many attributes. Therefore, if you are mapping two or more classes into one table, you will have to deal with database clutter.

In the next section, we'll discuss other strategies that might be a better fit for different scenarios.

Table per class strategy

As the name suggests, this strategy maps a table per entity class. In this case, the table itself is the discriminator, so all you need to do is set your inheritance strategy to the right value:

```
@Entity
@Inheritance(strategy=InheritanceType.TABLE_PER_CLASS)
public class Person {
...
}

@Entity
public class Driver extends Person {
...
}

@Entity
public class Passenger extends Person {
...
}
```

In this case, a Person class will be saved in the PERSON table, Driver in the DRIVER table, and Passenger in the PASSENGER table. This is a better strategy because you don't have the additional discriminator column and you are not leaving any holes in the table. However, you are still repeating the shared attributes of the parent class in all tables. So, each table will have all the columns that correspond to the attributes of the parent class. If this is not the desired structure either, you should consider the next strategy.

Joined strategy

If you use a joined strategy to support inheritance mapping, Hibernate stores the common attribute in one table and the attributes of the child class in a separate table with a foreign key reference to the parent table ID. Every child class gets a table. When the entity is read from database, Hibernate performs a left outer join operation on every table in the hierarchy to fetch the data. The SQL will look something similar to this (using the PostgreSQL dialect):

```
select
    person.id as id,
    person.firstname as firstname,
    person.lastname as lastname,
    passenger.DEST as DEST,
    driver.LIC_NUM as LIC_NUM,
    case
        when passenger.id is not null then 1
        when driver.id is not null then 2
        when person.id is not null then 0
    end as clazz_0_
from
    Person person
left outer join
    Passenger passenger
        on person.id=passenger.id
left outer join
    Driver driver
        on person.id=driver.id
where
    person.id=?
```

As you can see, in some cases the left outer joins may not be necessary, but Hibernate can't make this distinction and has to include every table mapping a subclass in the hierarchy.

Enumeration and custom data type

In this section, we see how to map "constants" to enumerated types. Constants are considered a small finite set of data elements, such as gender (Male, Female) or days of the week, such as Monday, Tuesday, and so on. Hibernate supports using enumerated types for mapping database columns containing data in a finite closed set. (The definition of a closed set comes straight from set theory.)

If you don't wish to use enumerated types, you can create a custom data type to map your data to a primitive type in Java, and you'll see that after we discuss the enumerated type.

Enumerated type

You can define an enumeration in Java and let Hibernate handle the mapping of "constants". JPA supports two kinds of enum: ORDINAL and STRING. If you use the ORDINAL enumeration type, the data in the mapped column is assumed to be an integer. You can guess how the STRING enumeration type behaves:

```
public enum WeekDay {
   Monday, Tuesday, Wednesday, Thursday, Friday, Saturday, Sunday
}


@Entity
public class WorkSchedule {
   @Id
   @GeneratedValue
   private long id;

   private Timestamp startTime;
   private Timestamp endTime;

   @Enumerated(EnumType.STRING)
   private WeekDay workDay;

   // getters and setters
}
```

The ORDINAL enumeration type starts from zero; Monday is 0 and Sunday is 6.

Custom data type mapping

As we discussed in the previous chapter, Hibernate loads type handlers at startup for a specific dialect. You can further create custom maps to map data in the database to primitive types in Java.

Hibernate has built-in types that map the true_false or yes_no values to Java types, such as Boolean. You can create your own user-defined types and use them in your application. Let's assume that the data in the database is for Spanish-speaking users, "Y" and "N" (for Yes and No) are stored as "S" and "N" (for Sí and No), and you wish to map this to a Boolean.

To define the type, implement a new class, as follows:

```
public class SpanishBoolean  extends AbstractSingleColumnStandardBasi
cType<Boolean>
                implements PrimitiveType<Boolean>,
DiscriminatorType<Boolean>
{
    private static final long serialVersionUID = 1L;
    public static final SpanishBoolean INSTANCE = new
SpanishBoolean();


    public SpanishBoolean() {
            super( CharTypeDescriptor.INSTANCE, new
BooleanTypeDescriptor('S', 'N') );
    }
    @Override
    public String getName() {
            return "si_no";
    }
    @Override
    public Class getPrimitiveClass() {
            return boolean.class;
    }
    @Override
    public Boolean stringToObject(String xml) throws Exception {
            return fromString( xml );
    }
    @Override
    public Serializable getDefaultValue() {
            return Boolean.FALSE;
    }
    @Override
    public String objectToSQLString(Boolean value, Dialect dialect)
    throws Exception {
            return StringType.INSTANCE.objectToSQLString( value ? "S"
: "N", dialect );
    }
}
```

Then, at startup, register the new type with the configuration:

```
Configuration configuration = new Configuration().configure();
configuration.registerTypeOverride(new SpanishBoolean());
```

Now, you are ready to use this in your entity:

```
@Entity
public class Persona {
   ...
   @Type(type="com.package.type.SpanishBoolean")
   private Boolean maestro;
}
```

When you save this entity, the `maestro` column will have a value of `S`, if `true`, or `N`, if `false`.

Summary

This chapter presented the foundation of object-relational mapping. We discussed the definition of an owner entity. We also defined value types and showed you how to map these properly in the entity table or a separate table. You also learned the concepts around ID generation and how to N generate ID using JPA or Hibernate strategies. You combined the value types and ID generation to discuss composite IDs.

Furthermore, we discussed associations and their cardinalities, one-to-one, many-to-one, and many-to-many, and showed you how to map self-referencing tables. Later we showed how to instruct Hibernate to perform cascade operations on associated entities.

We also covered inheritance and how Hibernate handles them. We showed you various strategies that can be used to handle inheritance. Finally, we showed you how to map enumerated types as well as create your own custom data type mapping.

In the next chapter, we will discuss more annotations to support more advanced mapping as well as the ones that affect database queries and the ones that affect the behaviour of an object. We'll also show you many Hibernate annotations that are not available in JPA.

3
Working with Annotations

In this chapter, we will look at various annotations and how they are used. Most Hibernate and JPA annotations were created for a specific purpose. For that reason, annotations discussed in this chapter are grouped together according to what they are used for. Some annotations are specified in JPA and some are only available in Hibernate. We will mostly focus on Hibernate annotations, specifically the ones that are not documented well or may be tricky to use. The discussion on annotations is grouped based on the following:

- Mapping and association
- Behavior
- The SQL/DDL modifier

You may have noticed that so far we have avoided the Hibernate configuration file and mostly focused on annotations. This is actually the goal throughout this book, since most developers prefer using annotations. In this chapter, we will pay closer attention to some important annotations.

Mapping and association

In the previous chapter, we demonstrated many annotations that defined mapping and associations between objects; most of those are JPA annotations. In this section, we will look at more annotations that affect mapping and associations. Most of these are only available in Hibernate, but we also cover some very useful JPA annotations that you may not have used.

@Any and @ManyToAny

The @Any and @ManyToAny annotations are only available in Hibernate. They are defined to support polymorphism in Java, in the sense that a discriminator column determines the subclass of a parent class (or interface).

For instance, if you have a table with a discriminator column that helps distinguish one class from the other, you can use the @Any annotation to map the rows to the correct class. We will discuss @ManyToAny here, as @Any is well documented in Hibernate API JavaDoc, but in short, @Any is used for a one-to-one association.

Consider the following relations that keep track of a person's mode of transportation throughout the travel itinerary, using a single table strategy:

TRAVELER

ID	FIRSTNAME	LASTNAME
1	David	Smith

TRAVELER_TRANSPORTATION

TRAVELER_ID	TRANSPORTATION_ID
1	2
1	3

TRANSPORTATION

DTYPE	ID	COST	DROPOFF	PICKUP	ARRIVAL	DEPARTURE
C	2	350	Baltimore	Washington		
A	3	500			JFK	BWI

The DTYPE column helps Hibernate determine which class to instantiate when it reads the data from the database, and this can be implemented as shown in the following listing:

```
@Entity
public class Traveler {
  @Id
  @GeneratedValue
  private long id;

  private String firstname;
  private String lastname;

  @ManyToAny(metaColumn=@Column(name="dtype"))
```

```
    private Set<Transportation> transportation =
                      new HashSet<Transportation>();

    // getters and setters
}

@Entity
@Inheritance(strategy=InheritanceType.SINGLE_TABLE)
@DiscriminatorColumn(name="dtype")
public class Transportation {
    @Id
    @GeneratedValue
    private long id;
    private double cost;
}

@Entity
@DiscriminatorValue(value="C")
public class Car extends Transportation {
    private String pickupLocation;
    private String dropOffLocation;
}

@Entity
@DiscriminatorValue(value="A")
public class Airplane extends Transportation {
    private String departureAirport;
    private String arrivalAirport;
}
```

You might have noticed that this looks awfully similar to the way we implemented inheritance, and you don't see the value in having the @ManyToAny annotation. In this case, the @ManyToAny annotation really acts like a @OneToMany, while supporting inheritance, as described in the preceding chapter. But the true purpose of the @Any annotations is actually to support polymorphism.

In Java, the notions of *inheritance* and *polymorphism* are closely related, but they are not quite the same. Think of polymorphism as implementing one or more interfaces, and inheritance is simply a class extending another, which is different from implementing an interface. Since Java doesn't support multiple-inheritance, and in order for your class to respond to multiple method calls, it needs to implement multiple Interfaces to be polymorphic.

So, how do you actually support polymorphic behavior using Hibernate? The answer is using the @Any annotations, as shown in the listing. Here, since we are dealing with a one-to-many association, we use @ManyToAny. If this were a one-to-one association, we could simply use the @Any annotation, as described in the JavaDoc:

```
@Entity
public class Traveler {
  @Id
  @GeneratedValue
  private long id;

private String firstname;
  private String lastname;

  @ManyToAny(metaColumn=@Column(name="trans_mode"))
  @AnyMetaDef(
           idType="long",
           metaValues = {
                   @MetaValue( value="C", targetEntity=Car.class ),
                   @MetaValue( value="A", targetEntity=Airplane.class
),
           },
           metaType = "char"
     )
  @JoinTable(
           name="traveler_transportation",
           joinColumns = @JoinColumn( name="traveler_id"),
           inverseJoinColumns = @JoinColumn( name="mode_id")
     )
  private Set<Transportation> transportation = new
    HashSet<Transportation>();

  // getters and setters
}

public interface Transportation {
  public double calculateCost();
}

@Entity
public class Car implements Transportation {
  @Id
  @GeneratedValue
  private long id;
```

```
    private String pickupLocation;
    private String dropOffLocation;
    // don't forget to implement equals and hashCode
}

@Entity
public class Airplane implements Transportation {
    @Id
    @GeneratedValue
    private long id;
    private String departureAirport;
    private String arrivalAirport;
    // don't forget to implement equals and hashCode
}
```

The trans_mode column is now the discriminator column. So, the tables now look different, as shown here:

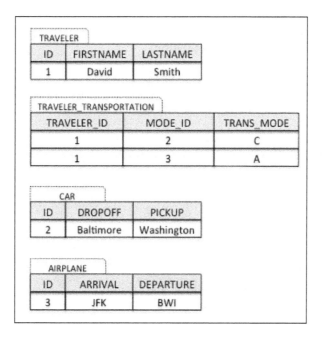

@MapsId

This annotation is a JPA annotation and is very useful to associate two entities (in separate tables) while one of them has a composite ID that includes the ID of the other entity. It can be used for one-to-one or many-to-one relationships. But there is a catch! In some cases, Hibernate doesn't populate the ID fields. Consider the following tables where you have a join table, called ENROLMENT, which associates a student with a course:

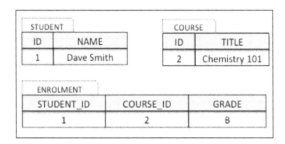

You can use the @MapsId annotation to map these relations and associations in Hibernate, as shown in the following listing:

```
@Entity
public class Student {
  @Id
  @GeneratedValue
  private long id;
  private String name;
}

@Entity
public class Course {
  @Id
  @GeneratedValue
  private long id;
  private String title;
}

@Embeddable
public class EnrolmentId implements Serializable {
  private long studentId;
  private long courseId;
  // don't forget equals() and hashCode() methods.
}
```

```
@Entity
public class Enrolment {

    @EmbeddedId
    private EnrolmentId id;
    private String grade;

    @MapsId("id")
    @OneToOne
    @JoinColumn(name="studentId")
    private Student student;

    @MapsId("id")
    @OneToOne
    @JoinColumn(name="courseId")
    private Course course;
}
```

But when you try to save these entities, you need to explicitly set the ID for the
`Enrolment` entity before attempting to save it:

```
session.save(student);
session.save(course);
EnrolmentId id = new EnrolmentId();
id.setCourseId(course.getId());
enrollment.setId(id);
session.save(enrollment);
```

This solution is not desired, and in fact, you may discover that `@MapsId` has caused a
lot of grief to Hibernate users. Luckily, there is another solution that is only supported
by Hibernate and doesn't work in JPA. You can declare your association in the
embedded `ID` class; in this case, you can add the `Student` and `Course` (one-to-one)
associations to the `EnrolmentId` class instead of the `Enrolment` class:

```
@Embeddable
public class EnrolmentId implements Serializable {
    @OneToOne
    @JoinColumn(name = "studentId")
    private Student student;

    @OneToOne
    @JoinColumn(name = "courseId")
    private Course course;
    // don't forget equals() and hashCode()
}
```

Note that the composite IDs, `studentId` and `courseId`, are no longer needed, and when you save your entities, you don't have to manually set the IDs, as they are generated for the `Student` and `Course` entities. Hibernate will map enrolments correctly based on those IDs.

@Fetch

Another useful Hibernate annotation is `@Fetch`, which can be used for instructing Hibernate to use a certain strategy when fetching the associated entities/collections. This is slightly different from the `FetchType` modifier (`LAZY`, `EAGER`) that you can specify, for example, on a `@OneToMany` annotation, in that you can specify three different fetching modes, `JOIN`, `SELECT`, and `SUBSELECT`. We will cover this in the next chapter.

@OrderBy

This annotation exists in both Hibernate and JPA. But in the JPA version, the syntax needs to be in JPQL. The Hibernate version of this annotation expects the `orderBy` clause to be in SQL. There are several annotations that exist in both Hibernate and JPA, such as `Entity`. So when you import these annotations, carefully choose the correct one from the package you want.

@ElementCollection and @CollectionTable

These two annotations are new and were introduced in JPA 2.0. They are worth mentioning here because they can be used in lieu of the `@OneToMany` annotation when the owned entity is a primitive type or an embeddable object.

If your entity is associated with a collection of primitive data type, you only need to use `@ElementCollection`. In this case, Hibernate will create an additional table to store the associated data, for instance, for the following example, Hibernate will create a table called `person` for the `Person` entity, another table called `person_aliases` to store the aliases for each person, and a table called `person_addresses` to store the addresses for a person as shown here. (An address is simply an embeddable class):

```
@Entity
public class Person {
  @Id
  @GeneratedValue
  private long id;
  private String firstname;
```

```
    private String lastname;

    @ElementCollection
    private List<String> aliases = new ArrayList<String>();

    @ElementCollection
    private List<Address> addresses = new ArrayList<Address>();
    // getters and setters
}
```

If you want additional control over the table name or the join columns, you can use `@CollectionTable`. The JPA documentation is quite good on this.

Behavior

In this section, we look at those annotations that affect the behavior of the entity.

@Cache

When you enable second-level cache, you can mark an entity as cacheable. In JPA, you can't specify a strategy, and the only strategy that is supported is READ_ONLY; refer to `@Cacheable` in JPA docs. Hibernate offers the capability to specify other strategies, besides READ_ONLY. We will see more on this in *Chapter 5, Hibernate Cache*.

@Access

The `@Access` annotation is a JPA annotation and is used to specify how to access a class field. By default, fields are accessed directly, typically using reflection, depending on the visibility of a field. But in some cases, you may want to perform additional work in the property accessor methods, such as getters and setters. In that case, you can instruct JPA (in this case, Hibernate) to not access the fields directly and use the accessor methods instead. (Refer to the access method of `field` and `property` in the JavaBeans™ specifications.)

You can annotate the `class` field or the class itself. If you use this annotation at the class level, it will apply to all the fields, including the ID. For this reason, you can't use generated IDs, and you will have to set the ID for this entity manually, which might be desirable in some cases. If that's not desirable, you should simply annotate the fields whose access type should be set accordingly.

Here is a sample listing that shows the `@Access` annotation used at the class level. Note, in this case, the `@Id` annotation must be applied to the getter method of ID:

```
@Entity
@Access(AccessType.PROPERTY)
public class Course {
  private long id;
  private String title;

  @Id
  public long getId() {
    return id;
  }
  // Other getters and setters
}
```

The following sample code shows the same annotation applied to select fields:

```
@Entity
public class Course {
  @Id
  @GeneratedValue
  private long id;

  @Access(AccessType.PROPERTY)
  private String title;

  // getters and setters as usual
}
```

@Cascade

This `@Cascade` annotation is similar to the cascade type you would define for one-to-one or one-to-many associations in JPA. However, it provides cascade behavior for query operations that are not supported in JPA, such as native `delete`, `lock`, `detach`, `replicate`, or `SaveOrUpdate`. Using `@Cascade`, you can propagate the native operations to the associated entities.

@CreationTimestamp and @UpdateTimestamp

The `@CreationTimestamp` and `@UpdateTimestamp` Hibernate annotations are used for fields whose types can be used as timestamps, for example, `Date`, `Calendar`, and `Timestamp`. Both annotations use the current date/time provided by the runtime JVM. The creation timestamp is set when you call `session.save()` or `session.saveOrUpdate()`, but when this is an existing object, the creation timestamp is not set at update time.

One interesting feature is that when you use these annotations, you don't need accessor methods such as getters and setters. (Unless you wish to fetch the values and display to the user, such as in a report, in which case you only need a getter.) Hibernate sets the values for you both in Java and SQL.

@Filter and @FilterDef

The `@Filter` and `@FilterDef` Hibernate annotations allow you to dynamically apply filters to your entity, and because you can change the behavior of an entity dynamically, it is listed in this section. But in reality, this annotation modifies the SQL at runtime.

At first, you define the filter typically applied to collections, and then you can enable the filter when you open a new session. Next, you can set the parameters of the filters dynamically.

Consider the following entities:

```
@Entity
public class Student {
  @Id
  @GeneratedValue
  private long id;
  private String name;
  private char gender;
  // getters and setters
}

@Entity
@FilterDef(name="genderFilter",
    parameters=@ParamDef(name="gender", type="character"))
public class Course {
  @Id
  @GeneratedValue
```

```
    private long id;
    private String title;

    @OneToMany(cascade=CascadeType.ALL)
    @Filter (
      name="genderFilter",
      condition="gender = :gender"
    )
    private Set<Student> students = new HashSet<Student>();
    // getters and setters
}
```

The Course entity includes a filter definition to associate with students based on their gender. By default, all filters are disabled. So, all students associated with this course will be returned. However, you can activate the filters as shown in the following listing:

```
Filter filter = session.enableFilter("genderFilter");
filter.setParameter("gender", 'F');
Course course = (Course) session.get(Course.class, courseId);
Set<Student> students = course.getStudents();
```

You can enable filters only on open sessions and after a transaction has begun.

@Immutable

The @Immutatble Hibernate annotation allows you to protect your entities from accidental updates. When you mark an entity as immutable, Hibernate will quietly ignore any update to the entity without any errors or exceptions. But if you apply this annotation to a collection and try to add or remove from the collection, Hibernate will throw an exception.

This is a useful annotation to protect changes to the database, for example, for reference or static data. Alternatively, you can declare two flavors of the same entity, one mutable and another immutable, where the mutable flavor is used in the application's administration business logic and the immutable used for non-privileged users.

@Loader

The @Loader Hibernate annotation lets you override the SQL query used to fetch the data. It uses a named query to load the data (refer to @NamedQuery). We will see examples of this in the next chapter when we discuss fetching.

@NotFound

Most of the time, we develop new applications that replace an old one. But in most cases, the database schema and data remain unchanged because the effort to migrate the data to a new schema is costly and very risky. For this reason, you often have to deal with data integrity issues, for example, when you have to deal with a database that lacks proper referential constraints.

Hibernate offers this annotation to handle cases where you except an association, but it doesn't exist in the database. Note that this will not work for cases where Hibernate joins the two tables to fetch the two entities, because in that case the SQL `join` will return no results. In other words, this is useful when you use lazy fetch, or SELECT strategy.

To demonstrate this, consider the following relations:

COURSE			ENROLMENT	
ID	TITLE		STUDENT_ID	COURSE_ID
2	Physics101		3	1
			4	1
			5	1

Notice that there is no row for a course whose ID is 1. So the referential integrity of this data has been compromised. If you don't use the @NotFound annotation, Hibernate will throw an exception by default when you try to fetch an enrolment entity from the database. You can suppress this exception as shown in the code listing:

```
@Entity
public class Course {
  @Id
  @GeneratedValue
  private long id;
  private String title;

  @OneToMany(mappedBy="course")
  private Set<StudentEnrolment> students = new
    HashSet<StudentEnrolment>();
  // getters and setters
}

@Entity
public class StudentEnrolment {
```

```
    @Id
    @GeneratedValue
    @Column(name="student_id")
    private long studentId;

    @ManyToOne
    @NotFound(action=NotFoundAction.IGNORE)
    Course course;
    // getters and setters
}
```

The default value for NotFoundAction is EXCEPTION, which causes an exception to be thrown. This is recommended by the Hibernate team, but clearly it depends on your use case.

@SortComparator and @SortNatural

The @SortComparator and @SortNatural annotations only exist in Hibernate and they are used to sort a collection in memory, as opposed to adding the order by clause to the SQL. You may not use both annotations together; it's one or the other. Here, we show an example of how to use @SortComparator:

```
@Entity
public class Team {
  @Id
  @GeneratedValue
  private long id;

  @OneToMany(cascade=CascadeType.ALL)
  @SortComparator(value=PersonComparator.class)
  private Set<Person> persons = new HashSet<Person>();
  // getters and setters
}

@Entity
public class Person {
  @Id
  @GeneratedValue
  private long id;
  private String firstname;
  private String lastname;
  // getters and setters
}
```

```
public class PersonComparator implements Comparator<Person> {
  @Override
  public int compare(Person p1, Person p2) {
    if (p1.getLastname().equals(p2.getLastname())) {
    return p1.getFirstname().compareTo(p2.getFirstname());
    }
    return p1.getLastname().compareTo(p2.getLastname());
  }
}
```

The order of the persons without the sort will be like this:

```
Person [id=3, firstname=Adam, lastname=Smith]
Person [id=2, firstname=David, lastname=Smith]
Person [id=4, firstname=David, lastname=Brown]
```

However, if you add the Sort annotation (with the comparator), the order will be as follows:

```
Person [id=4, firstname=David, lastname=Brown]
Person [id=3, firstname=Adam, lastname=Smith]
Person [id=2, firstname=David, lastname=Smith]
```

Lastly, note that for the preceding example, I used HashSet. This works only if you are just reading the related entities and wish to sort them in memory. On the other hand, if you wish to use the same entity to write to the database, you will need to use a sorted set type for the collection.

SQL/DDL modifier

In this section, we will discuss annotations that modify the SQL or the DDL used by Hibernate to perform a query or generate schema objects. The DDL modifying annotations are important if you use Hibernate to generate your tables.

@Check

Using the @Check Hibernate annotation, you can add the CHECK constraints to your table. The constraint defined in the @Check annotation uses the syntax that is supported by the database of your choice.

The following listing adds a constraint to the price column:

```
@Entity
@Check(constraints = "price >= 0")
public class Item {
```

```
    @Id
    @GeneratedValue
    private long id;
    private String description;
    private double price;
    // setters and getters
}
```

The DDL generated using PostgreSQL, is shown here:

```
create table Item (
    id int8 not null,
    description varchar(255),
    price float8 not null,
    primary key (id),
    check (price >= 0)
)
```

@ColumnDefault

Another DDL modifier is the Hibernate annotation @ColumnDefault that adds a default value to a column when the DDL is generated:

```
@Entity
public class Address {
  @Id
  @GeneratedValue
  private long id;

  private String street;
  private String city;
  @ColumnDefault(value="'US'")
  private String country;
  // getters and setters
}
```

This results in the following DDL:

```
create table Address (
    id int8 not null,
    city varchar(255),
    country varchar(255) default 'US',
    street varchar(255),
    primary key (id)
)
```

@ColumnTransformer

The `@ColumnTransformer` Hibernate annotation is very useful for manipulating the SQL to perform additional transformation on a column, both at the time of read and write. It modifies the question mark placeholders in the prepared statement of JDBC per the values in this annotation.

In the following example, both the first and last names are converted to uppercase letters at the time of read from and write to the database. (This is useful for implementing case-insensitive text):

```
@Entity
public class Person {
  @Id
  @GeneratedValue
  private long id;
  @ColumnTransformer(read=("upper(firstname)"),
    write=("upper(?)"))
  private String firstname;
  @ColumnTransformer(read=("upper(lastname)"), write=("upper(?)"))
  private String lastname;
  // getters and setters
}
```

Note that both the `read` and `write` must follow your database syntax. With this annotation, you can perform many clever tricks using low-level SQL syntax.

@DynamicInsert and @DynamicUpdate

The `@DynamicInsert` and `@DynamicUpdate` annotations only exist in Hibernate. When used, Hibernate will generate the SQL only for the columns that are not null. This offers an improvement for tables that have many nullable columns that don't always get set at insert or update time.

Consider the following listing:

```
@Entity
@DynamicInsert
@DynamicUpdate
public class Person {
  @Id
  @GeneratedValue
  private long id;
```

```
    private String firstname;
    private String lastname;
    // getters and setters
}
```

If you only populate the value of firstname, Hibernate will create the SQL for non-null columns:

```
insert
into
    Person
    (firstname, id)
values
    (?, ?)
```

Otherwise, the SQL will look like this:

```
insert
into
    Person
    (firstname, lastname, id)
values
    (?, ?, ?)
```

It is highly recommended to use these two annotations for tables that have many columns that don't get updated often.

@Formula

This @Formula Hibernate annotation is very similar to @ColumnTransformer, except that it only works on read, and doesn't have write capabilities. If you don't need the write capabilities, you should use @Formula.

@SelectBeforeUpdate

This @SelectBeforeUpdate annotation is only available in Hibernate and its purpose is to prevent unnecessary updates to the database. If you enable this on an entity, before any update operation, Hibernate performs a select and compares what's in the session to. what's in the database. If they are different, Hibernate will perform the update. Obviously, this will cost you an extra trip to the database, but it might be useful in certain cases. For example, if your update statement fires a database trigger or an event, it may be undesirable if no updates are made to the values.

@SQLDelete and @Where

There are times when we don't wish to delete an entity by removing the row from the table. In such cases, we may just want to mark the record as deleted. This is called a **soft delete**. The @SQLDelete Hibernate annotation can help you achieve this. It is typically accompanied with a @Where annotation that's needed to filter out the non-deleted rows using the provided SQL clause.

> The deleted column is declared as Boolean in PostgreSQL, the database used to demonstrate this example, and Hibernate was incorrectly thinking that FALSE was a column name and adding table alias prefix to it, as in person0_.deleted = person0_. FALSE, and that's why single quotes are used to prevent Hibernate from doing that. Luckily, PostgreSQL is generous enough to accept a Boolean value quoted or unquoted. Your mileage may vary depending on your choice of the database.

A sample usage is shown in the following listing:

```
@Entity
@SQLDelete(sql="UPDATE person SET deleted = TRUE WHERE id = ?")
@Where(clause="deleted = 'FALSE'")
public class Person {
  @Id
  @GeneratedValue
  private long id;
  private String firstname;
  private String lastname;
  private boolean deleted;
  @UpdateTimestamp
  private Date updateTime;
  // getters and setters
}
```

Note that this entity has a field called updateTime, which is annotated with @UpdateTimestamp. This was intentionally added to demonstrate that in this case Hibernate would not update the timestamp column for you automatically, because when you use this annotation, you effectively force Hibernate to execute the SQL that you provide. So, if you wish to update the timestamp column, you would have to add that to your update statement.

@SQLInsert and @SQLUpdate

Similar to the SQL `Delete` statement, Hibernate also offers other annotations to support custom `Insert` and `Update` SQL statements. These two annotations are worth considering in some cases. Their usage is simple, so we will not provide a sample listing. However, they are included here to bring them to your attention.

@SubSelect and @Synchronize

The `@SubSelect` and `@Synchronize` Hibernate annotations and are very useful to create an immutable entity, typically a collection, from a custom SQL statement. The easiest way to think about this is to think of it as a view from one or more tables. The idea is that you map your entity to an SQL statement, a Subselect, and just perform fetch operations on that entity.

Suppose you have two tables, each of which has its own corresponding JPA entity. If you need an entity that is a `summary` view of the joined relationship between these two tables, you can do this using a Sub-Select entity. To demonstrate this, consider the following relations that keep track of a person information as well as their experience with programming languages and when they used it:

PERSON

ID	FIRSTNAME	LASTNAME	...	...	...
1	James	Dean	...	...	...

LANGUAGE

ID	NAME	YEAR	PERSON_ID	...	...	...
2	Java	2015	1	...	...	...
3	PHP	2014	1	...	...	...
4	Ruby	2013	1	...	...	...
5	Java	2012	1	...	...	...

As the figure suggests, these two relations may have many columns that might not be interesting in some cases. One thing you can do is to create a VIEW in the database and map an entity to that view. But in most cases, database schema changes are very difficult to make due to governance and policies.

You can create your own view in Hibernate and just select the columns from these two tables in which you are interested, as demonstrated in the following listing:

```
@Entity
public class Person {
```

```
    @Id
    @GeneratedValue
    private long id;
    private String firstname;
    private String lastname;
    @UpdateTimestamp
    private Date updateTime;
    // getters and setters
}

@Entity
public class Language {
  @Id
  @GeneratedValue
  private long id;
  private String name;
  private long year;
  @ManyToOne
  private Person person;
  // getters and setters
}

@Entity
@Subselect("select row_number() over() as id, "
    + "   p.firstname, p.lastname, l.name as language, "
    + "   max(l.year) as lastused, count(*) as numyears "
    + "from person p join language l " + "on p.id = l.person_id "
    + "group by p.firstname, p.lastname, l.name")
@Synchronize({ "person", "language" })
public class Experience {
  @Id
  private long id;
  private String firstname;
  private String lastname;
  private String language;
  private long lastUsed;
  private long numYears;
  // getters and setters
}
```

There are a few interesting things to note. First, the column names of the resulting relation match those of the class fields. Second, this uses a built-in PostgreSQL `row_number()` to generate a row ID and that is mapped to the entity ID. You don't have to do this, you could designate one or more columns to uniquely identify a row. If you use more than one column for ID, you need to use a composite ID in your entity. Next, note how the SQL includes aggregate functions such as max, count, group by, and so on. This indicates that you have a lot of freedom in composing this query; after all, it is native query.

Finally, let's talk a bit about `@Synchronize`. This tells Hibernate that before executing this query, any entity in the session that maps to those tables must be synchronized with the database, that is, flushed. That's because if Hibernate doesn't flush the entities, you may not get the correct result.

To use this entity in your main code, you simply use an HQL statement similar to the following:

```
List<Experience> resume = session.createQuery("from Experience").
list();
```

@WhereJoinTable

The `@WhereJoinTable` Hibernate annotation adds the `where` clause to the `@JoinTable` annotation, which is a JPA annotation. We covered join tables, which is a relation that maps the ID from one table to the ID of another table to create the association. In some cases, besides the two ID columns, you may have other columns in the join table. You can use this annotation to further limit the query results.

@NaturalId

We mentioned in an earlier chapter that new versions of Hibernate require that each entity has an ID to uniquely identify a row in a table, even if this identification is meaningless to your problem domain. Your ID column will have a unique and not-null constraint.

While the entity ID is considered to be a surrogate key for the most part, you can still designate other fields to be natural keys for your entity/record. This will have the benefit of adding a unique and not-null constraint to the DDL to further strengthen your data integrity. And you can do this by annotating the appropriate fields with `@NaturalId` annotation.

Summary

We demonstrated many annotations and why and how they are used. The previous chapter covered mapping concepts; we continued that discussion in this chapter by looking at annotations that help us create better object/relational mapping. We also looked at annotations that impact the behavior of an entity. Finally, we looked at annotations that modify the SQL statement that is composed by Hibernate.

As mentioned earlier, we will use mostly annotations in this book, whenever possible. In the next chapter, we will explore various ways of fetching the data from the database and discuss different strategies.

4
Advanced Fetching

In this chapter, we will discuss various ways to fetch the data from the permanent store. In previous chapters, we have already seen some ways to fetch the data when working with annotated entities. Now, we will focus a little more on the annotations that are related to data fetch, **Hibernate Query Language (HQL)**, execution of native SQL, criteria objects, and filters. We will also demonstrate how to perform pagination, which is a functionality that's very common in most enterprise applications.

We will cover the following topics in this chapter:

- Fetching strategies
- Hibernate Query Language
- Native SQL
- Criteria objects
- Filters
- Pagination

Fetching strategy

In **Java Persistence API (JPA)**, you can provide a hint to fetch the data *lazily* or *eagerly* using the `FetchType` implementation. However, some implementations may ignore the lazy strategy and just fetch everything eagerly. Hibernate's default to reduce the memory footprint of your application is `FetchType.LAZY`.

The lazy and eager strategies impact the associated entity. When you set fetch strategy of an associated entity to lazy, Hibernate will not fetch the associated entity until you access the associated entity. You must access the associated entity in the same session where you fetched the parent entity; otherwise, you will encounter an exception. On the other hand, the eager fetch strategy forces Hibernate to retrieve the associated entity when the parent entity is fetched.

As mentioned in the previous chapter, Hibernate offers additional fetch modes in addition to the commonly-used JPA fetch types. Here, we will discuss how they are related and provide an explanation so that you understand when to use which.

The JOIN fetch mode

The JOIN fetch type forces Hibernate to create a SQL join statement to populate both the entities and their related entities using just one SQL statement. However, the JOIN fetch mode also implies that the fetch type is EAGER, so there is no need to specify the fetch type.

To understand this better, consider the following classes:

```
@Entity
public class Course {
  @Id
  @GeneratedValue
  priva
  te long id;
  private String title;

  @OneToMany(cascade=CascadeType.ALL, mappedBy="course")
  @Fetch(FetchMode.JOIN)
  private Set<Student> students = new HashSet<Student>();

  // getters and setters
}

@Entity
public class Student {

  @Id
  @GeneratedValue
  private long id;
  private String name;
```

```
    private char gender;

    @ManyToOne
    private Course course;

    // getters and setters
}
```

In this case, we are instructing Hibernate to use JOIN to fetch Course and Student in one SQL statement. This is the SQL that is composed by Hibernate:

```
select
    course0_.id as id1_0_0_,
    course0_.title as title2_0_0_,
    students1_.course_id as course_i4_0_1_,
    students1_.id as id1_1_1_,
    students1_.gender as gender2_1_2_,
    students1_.name as name3_1_2_
from
    Course course0_
left outer join
    Student students1_
        on course0_.id=students1_.course_id
where
    course0_.id=?
```

As you can see, Hibernate uses left join for all courses and any students that may have signed up for these courses. Another important thing to note is that if you use HQL, Hibernate will ignore JOIN fetch mode, and you'll have to specify the join in the HQL. (We will discuss HQL in the next section.) In other words, let's suppose that you fetch a course entity using a statement, such as the following:

```
List<Course> courses = session
        .createQuery("from Course c where c.id = :courseId")
        .setLong("courseId", chemistryId)
        .list();
```

In this case, Hibernate will use SELECT mode. But if you don't use HQL, as shown here, Hibernate will pay attention to the fetch mode instructions that are provided by the annotation:

```
Course course = (Course) session.get(Course.class, chemistryId);
```

The SELECT fetch mode

In the SELECT fetch mode, Hibernate uses an additional SELECT statement to fetch the related entities. This mode doesn't affect the behavior of the fetch type (LAZY or EAGER), so they will work as expected. To demonstrate this, consider the same example that was used in the last section, and let's examine the output, as follows:

```
select id, title
from Course
where id=?

select course_if, id, gender, name
from Student
where course_id=?
```

Note that first, Hibernate fetches and populates the Course entity and then uses the course ID to fetch the related students. Of course, if your fetch type is set to LAZY and you never referenced the related entities, the second SELECT is never executed.

The SUBSELECT fetch mode

The SUBSELECT fetch mode is used to minimize the number of SELECT statements that are executed to fetch the related entities. If you first fetch the owner entities and then try to access the associated owned entities without SUBSELECT, Hibernate will issue an additional SELECT statement for every one of the owner entities.

Using SUBSELECT, you instruct Hibernate to use a SQL subselect to fetch all the owners for the list of owned entities that are already fetched.

To understand this better, let's explore the following entity classes:

```
@Entity
public class Owner {
  @Id
  @GeneratedValue
  private long id;
  private String name;

  @OneToMany(cascade=CascadeType.ALL, mappedBy="owner")
  @Fetch(FetchMode.SUBSELECT)
  private Set<Car> cars = new HashSet<Car>();
  // getters and setters
}
```

```
@Entity
public class Car {
  @Id
  @GeneratedValue
  private long id;
  private String model;

  @ManyToOne
  private Owner owner;
  // getters and setters
}
```

If you try to fetch from the `Owner` table, Hibernate will only issue two select statements, one to fetch the `owners` entity and another to fetch the `cars` entity for these owners using a subselect, as shown here:

```
select
    id, name
from
    Owner

select
    owner_id,
    id,
    model
from
    Car
where
    owner_id in (select id from Owner)
```

Without the SUBSELECT fetch mode, instead of the second select statement, as shown in the preceding code, Hibernate would execute a `select` statement for every entity returned by the first statement. This is known as the *n+1* problem, where one SELECT statement is executed, and then for each returned entity, another SELECT statement is executed to fetch the associated entities.

Finally, the SUBSELECT fetch mode is not supported in *ToOne* associations, such as *OneToOne* or *ManyToOne*, because it was designed for relationships where the ownership of the entities is clear.

Batch fetching

Another strategy offered by Hibernate is batch fetching. This is very similar to SUBSELECT except that instead of using SUBSELECT, the entity IDs are explicitly listed in the SQL, and the list size is determined by the @BatchSize annotation. This may perform slightly better for smaller batches. (Keep in mind that all commercial database engines also perform query optimization.)

To demonstrate this, let's consider the following entity classes:

```
@Entity
public class Owner {
  @Id
  @GeneratedValue
  private long id;
  private String name;

  @OneToMany(cascade=CascadeType.ALL, mappedBy="owner")
  @BatchSize(size=10)
  private Set<Car> cars = new HashSet<Car>();
  // getters and setters
}

@Entity
public class Car {
  @Id
  @GeneratedValue
  private long id;
  private String model;

  @ManyToOne
  private Owner owner;
  // getters and setters
}
```

Using @BatchSize, we instruct Hibernate to fetch the related entities (cars) using a SQL statement that uses a "where in" clause, which lists the relevant ID for the owner entity:

```
select
    id, name
from
    Owner

select
```

```
    owner_id, id, model
from
    Car
where
    owner_id in (?, ?)
```

In this case, the first select statement only returned two rows. But if this returned more than the batch size, there would be multiple select statements to fetch the owned entities, each fetching 10 entities at a time.

Hibernate Query Language

Hibernate offers its own query language, called HQL, which resembles SQL in many ways but also supports additional features. There are some differences, for example, instead of the table name, you simply use the entity name and Hibernate will figure out the table name. This is because both HQL and **JPA Query Language** (**JPQL**) use an object model, and both languages are considered to be object-oriented and support polymorphism and inheritance concepts.

In this section, we'll focus on HQL and also how Hibernate supports native SQL. However, this section is not meant to be a language reference for HQL; this is indeed a powerful language and most likely deserves its own book. For now, it is highly recommended that you read the online documentations for a complete reference.

When composing HQL statements, you should be aware of the following:

- HQL is case insensitive, except when you are referring to entity classes. It's a convention to use lowercase for all HQL keywords and use uppercase when referring to entity classes.

- In more complex HQL statements, entities need to be aliased so that they can be referred to later in the statement.

- HQL doesn't automatically update the properties that are annotated with @UpdateTimestamp. You'll have to include the timestamp update in the HQL statement.

- Hibernate supports JPQL, but other JPA implementations may not support HQL.

- HQL offers various types of parameter binding supporting JDBC style, JPQL, and as well as its own, in the form of named and indexed parameters.

Fetch queries

Typically, you wouldn't use HQL to fetch an entity if you know its primary ID. For this reason, HQL is mostly used to fetch a collection of entities that meet a certain search criteria. For example, you can use HQL to search by the first letter of first name:

```
List<Person> persons = session
        .createQuery("from Person where firstname like 'J%'")
        .list();
```

Hibernate will convert this to the following SQL, which looks fairly similar:

```
select id, firstname, lastname from Person where firstname like 'J%'
```

Delete and update

Similar to fetch, you should only use HQL to perform bulk deletes and updates:

```
int numRecs = session
        .createQuery("delete from Person where lastname = 'Johnson'")
        .executeUpdate();
```

However, as you can see, you need to call the `executeUpdate()` method for both `delete` and `update` statements, which returns the number of records that are affected by the statements. However, keep in mind that this may not return the count of all the entities that are affected.

Join

As mentioned earlier in this chapter, by default, Hibernate uses the `lazy` fetch type. If you set the parent entity to eagerly fetch the related entities, Hibernate will also fetch them, even if you don't include the related entity in the HQL. However, this will execute an additional SQL for every parent entity that it fetches. To demonstrate this, let's consider the following entity classes:

```
@Entity
public class Person {
  @Id
  @GeneratedValue
  private long id;
  private String firstname;
  private String lastname;

  @OneToMany(cascade=CascadeType.ALL, mappedBy="person",
          fetch=FetchType.EAGER)
```

```
    @Fetch(FetchMode.JOIN)
    Set<Address> addresses = new HashSet<Address>();
    // getters and setters
}

@Entity
public class Address {
  @Id
  @GeneratedValue
  private long id;

  private String street;
  private String city;

  @ManyToOne
  private Person person;

  // getters and setters
}
```

Now, let's use HQL to fetch the `Person` entities:

```
persons = session
    .createQuery("from Person where lastname = 'Johnson'")
    .list();
```

This query returns all the matching `Person` entities, and then for each `Person` entity, an additional query is executed to get the related addresses (*n+1* queries) even if the fetch mode is set to `join`, as it is in this case.

To eliminate the *n+1* problem, we can use `Join` in HQL to fetch everything in one query. The `fetch` keyword in the HQL here instructs Hibernate to retrieve and initialize the associated entities (addresses) when the parent entity is fetched:

```
List<Person> persons = session
.createQuery("from Person p left join fetch p.addresses where
p.lastname = 'Johnson'")
.list();
```

It's worth noting a few things in this HQL. The first is the use of the `p` alias. This is needed because we are referring to the entity in other places in the HQL. Secondly, we join the `Person` and the `Address` table (using `left join`), so the query result will include all the columns from persons with their corresponding address. This is a cartesian product of both tables, which is then filtered by matching IDs between an address and a personal record. (It's also filtered by the last name in the `where` clause.)

Another important note is that the `addresses` property in the `Person` entity is being referenced directly. This way, Hibernate knows that you wish to make the join between these two tables, based on their primary key relationship. (Notice that in the `join` clause or the `where` clause, we are not specifying `person.id = address.person_id`; Hibernate does this for us because we are referring to `addresses` property of `Person`.)

Finally, the use of the `fetch` keyword tells Hibernate that we also want to fetch the addresses, and not just the `Person`, which is similar to an `eager` fetch.

The HQL translates to something that is similar to the following SQL:

```
select
    person0_.id,
    addresses1_.id as address_id,
    person0_.firstname,
    person0_.lastname,
    addresses1_.city,
    addresses1_.street,
    addresses1_.person_id
from
    Person person0_
left outer join
    Address addresses1_
        on person0_.id=addresses1_.person_id
where
    person0_.lastname='Johnson'
```

Native SQL

Native SQL statements are also supported in Hibernate, except you will need to use a different API call to compose a query object. There are mainly two reasons you would want to use a native SQL. The first is that you wish to use a specific feature offered by your database solution that may not be supported by Hibernate. The second is when you wish to execute an ad hoc query and store the result in an object that is not a Hibernate entity.

If you don't associate an entity with the query result, Hibernate returns the result set in a list of object array. This is known as a Scalar Query. However, you can associate an entity with the native query and Hibernate will return a list of this entity; this is known as Entity query. Let's see how these work.

Scalar query

When you execute a native SQL, the result of this query is returned in a list of object arrays. Consider the following query:

```
List<Object[]> objectList = session
.createSQLQuery("SELECT * FROM PERSON")
  .list();
```

Each element of the list is essentially a row returned from the query. Each element of the object array represents the value of a column.

Hibernate does a good job guessing the scalar data type and will instantiate the appropriate object to hold the value of each column. However, sometimes you may need to specify the type. You can do this by adding a scalar hint for each column you would like to return, as follows:

```
List<Object[]> objectList = session
.createSQLQuery("SELECT * FROM PERSON")
.addScalar("ID", LongType.INSTANCE)
.addScalar("FIRSTNAME", StringType.INSTANCE)
.addScalar("LASTNAME", StringType.INSTANCE)
.addScalar("BIRTHDATE", DateType.INSTANCE)
.list();
```

That way, you can safely cast the array elements:

```
for(Object[] objects: objectList) {
  Long id = (Long) objects[0];
  String firstname = (String) objects[1];
  String lastname = (String) objects[2];
  Date birthdate = (Date) objects[3];
}
```

Another advantage of adding scalar hints is that it instructs Hibernate to only fetch those columns, so even though you are selecting every column in your native SQL, Hibernate will only extract the values for the columns that are specified. (Please note that the SQL doesn't change, it still is SELECT *, so from a JDBC perspective it fetches all columns.)

Entity query

You can attach an entity to the native SQL and Hibernate will correctly populate this entity for you. The following code demonstrates how this works:

```
List<Person> persons = session
.createSQLQuery("SELECT * FROM PERSON")
.addEntity(Person.class)
.list();
```

Hibernate will return the results using the `Person` class.

It's even possible to join multiple tables and fetch the related entities. For example, you can join the `Person` table and the `Address` table to fetch all `Persons` with their associated `Address` entities:

```
String hql =
    "SELECT p.*, a.* FROM PERSON p, ADDRESS a " +
    "WHERE p.id = a.person_id";

List<Object[]> objectList = session
    .createSQLQuery(hql)
    .addEntity("p", Person.class)
    .addJoin("a", "p.addresses")
    .list();
```

It's worth noting a few things in the preceding code. The return type is a list of object arrays, this is because Hibernate will return the `Person` entity as the first element of `Object[]`, that is, `objectList[0]`, and `Address` entity as the second element of the array. Also, you may encounter duplicate entities in cases where the association is one to many. If you ever have to fetch the data this way, you may have to carefully extract and handle the root entities and their associated entities using your own code, after you fetch all the data.

Criteria objects

Another way to create a fetch query is using criteria objects. This is more in tune with the object-oriented mindset. However, the real advantage that this brings is that this makes composing dynamic queries easier.

Criteria queries are composed from an object graph, and as new search criteria are added, new objects (`Restrictions`, `Order`, and so on) are added to the graph. This is especially very useful when you are building a report or search screen in your application, for example, navigating through items in an online store.

In its simplest form, a `Criteria` object is created, as follows:

```
Criteria criteria = session.createCriteria(Person.class);
List<Person> persons = criteria.list();
```

In this case, the `Person` entity is configured to fetch the associated entities eagerly, and the criteria API follows this instruction.

You can further modify the `Criteria` object, for example, by adding a WHERE clause:

```
List<Person> persons = criteria
    .add(Restrictions.eq("lastname", "Johnson"))
    .list();
```

Or use a LIKE clause, as follows:

```
List<Person> persons = criteria
    .add(Restrictions.ilike("firstname", "M%"))
    .list();
```

> The `Restrictions` class also supports a `like` method, which acts similar to `ilike`. The latter was motivated by the `ilike` keyword in PostgreSQL, which performs a case insensitive pattern matching.

You can add order to the result set:

```
List<Person> persons = criteria
    .add(Restrictions.eq("lastname", "Johnson"))
    .addOrder(Order.asc("firstname"))
    .list();
```

If you know that your query is certain to return one row, for example, if you search by a natural key, such as Social Security Number (SSN) or e-mail address, then you can use the unique result method of `criteria`:

```
Criteria criteria = session.createCriteria(Person.class);
Person person = (Person) criteria
    .add(Restrictions.eqOrIsNull("ssn", ssn))
    .uniqueResult();
```

You can also add more criteria to the root criteria object graph to force a join so that you can search on the associated entities. For example, the following will return all `Person` entities that have an associated address whose city is set to `Fairfax`:

```
Criteria criteria = session.createCriteria(Person.class)
```

```
    .createCriteria("addresses");
  List<Person> persons = criteria
    .add(Restrictions.eq("city", "Fairfax"))
    .list();
```

One last important note to mention about the criteria API is that, similar to entity queries discussed earlier, in some cases this may return duplicate rows. So, you may have to perform some additional work in Java to get rid of duplicates. Throughout this book, we encourage you to implement the `equals` and `hashCode` method for your entities when applicable. This is one reason why these methods can be very useful. By adding your entities to a Set, you can quickly get rid of the duplicate entities.

The criteria API is quite rich and powerful. We highly recommend that you refer to the online documentation for further information.

Filters

In the previous chapter, we showed you how to apply filters using annotation. Another way is to apply filters to a collection that is already in the persistence context. This is quite useful to fetch only a subset of a collection.

For example, if you have a list of teachers and their students in the database and you are simply interested in fetching the records for all the female students, you can use filters, which can be very efficient in some cases.

To demonstrate how to use filters, let's assume that we have the following entities:

```
@Entity
public class Teacher {
  @Id
  @GeneratedValue
  private long id;
  private String name;

  @OneToMany(cascade=CascadeType.ALL)
  Set<Student> students = new HashSet<Student>();
  // getters and setters
}

@Entity
public class Student {
  @Id
  @GeneratedValue
  private long id;
```

```
    private String name;
    private String gender;
    // getters and setters
}
```

You can get the teacher record using a simple fetch:

```
Teacher teach = (Teacher) session
.get(Teacher.class, teacher.getId());
```

At this point, as we fetched lazily, we only have the uninitialized version of the associated student entities. Of course, as soon as we try to access the student set from the `teacher` entity, Hibernate will fire off a SQL to get all the student records. However, we are only interested in the female students. This is how you get the records of female students using filters:

```
List<Student> students = session
  .createFilter(teach.getStudents(),
    "select this where this.gender='female'")
  .list();
```

A few things are worth noting here. First, it doesn't matter if your root entity is set to fetch lazily or eagerly, either way the original collection, in this case students, is untouched and the result of the filter is a new collection. Second, Hibernate does not perform this in memory. It actually goes back to the database to execute an SQL for the filter. Finally, the second argument is HQL. The `this` special keyword refers to the element of the collection that is being acted on by the filter, in this case a student entity in the collection.

Pagination

Paginating through search data is a very common functionality in most enterprise applications. Luckily, Hibernate provides several ways of paginating through the data. One efficient way of doing this is by using the criteria objects that were discussed earlier.

Usually, pagination is accompanied by sorting the search results. The following example shows how this is done using the criteria API:

```
Criteria criteria = session.createCriteria(Person.class);
List<Person> persons = criteria
  .addOrder(Order.asc("lastname"))
  .setFirstResult(75)
  .setMaxResults(20)
  .list();
```

Hibernate (actually, the database dialect) composes the SQL to limit the result set to your max result, starting from the offset:

```
select <columns>
from
Person this_
left outer join
Address addresses_
    on this_.id=addresses_.person_id
order by
        this_.lastname asc limit ? offset ?
```

It is important to know that different database engines implement `limit` differently. The performance of your query can be impacted if the database doesn't stop processing the rows after the max result has been reached.

Summary

In this chapter, we covered many ways of fetching datasets from the database. You can use HQL, JPA, or even native SQL. We also showed you how to use the criteria API and further apply filters to collections. We also discussed fetching strategies and when each should be used. Finally, we discussed pagination, which is almost always a functional requirement.

In the next chapter, we will discuss the Hibernate cache, its architecture, strategies, and implementation.

5
Hibernate Cache

In this chapter, we will discuss various topics on Hibernate caching. One of the advantages of using Hibernate is its ability to cache entities to minimize trips to the database. Of course, to take advantage of this feature correctly, one must be fully aware of the pitfalls. For example, if you cache entities that can be updated by another application, then your cache may be invalid. In this chapter, we will discuss various cache levels, how to enable cache, strategies, and more:

- Cache structure:
    - Cache scope
    - First-level cache
    - Second-level cache
    - Query cache
- Caching benefits and pitfalls
- Caching strategies:
    - Read only
    - Non-strict read write
    - Read write
    - Transactional
    - Object identity
- Managing cache:
    - Remove cached entities
    - Cache modes
- Cache metrics

Cache structure

You may not have realized but you have already been using at least the first-level cache that is managed by the Hibernate session. In addition to the first-level cache, Hibernate also offers the ability to set up a second-level cache. Furthermore, it's possible to cache the result of queries that are frequently executed, which are known as query caches. Let's discuss these here.

Cache scope

Before we discuss cache levels, we need to understand the scope of a cached entity:

- A cached entity may only span the life of a **transaction**; this means the cached entity is only available for the thread that owns the persistence unit of work.

- The next wider scope is the **process**, for example, your web application. An entity may be cached as long as the web application is running. In this case, the cached entity may be shared by multiple threads, perhaps even concurrently.

- Finally, if you are in a clustered environment, entities can be cached on every node of the **cluster**. Clearly, when an entity changes, nodes have to be synchronized to ensure that the entities' values are the same across all the nodes.

Another important note to keep in mind is entity identity. The discussion that we had in *Chapter 1, Entity and Session* on object identity and equality is also relevant here. It should be evident that when you access a cached entity in a transaction scope cache, you get back the same entity every time by reference, which means two references to the same entity are equal both from the Java and Persistence perspective. This may not always be the case in the process scope cache, and it's never the case in the cluster scope cache. We will return to this when we discuss caching strategies later in this chapter.

First-level cache

When an entity is placed in the persistence context, it is cached until the session is closed or until the entity is evicted from the session. This is the first-level cache whose scope is the unit of work. This is also known as the transaction-level cache. Clearly, this does not apply to stateless sessions, which were discussed in *Chapter 1, Entity and Session*, because, as you may recall, a stateless session does not have a persistence context.

An important feature of the Hibernate first-level cache is automated dirty checking. Hibernate knows the state of each entity compared to its state in the database at the time when the entity was fetched from storage. If the state of the entity doesn't change during a persistence unit of work, Hibernate will not attempt to synchronize this entity with the database when session is flushed. Even if you modify an entity and then change it back to its original state, Hibernate is smart enough to determine that it doesn't need to be synchronized with the database because the original value was restored.

Furthermore, the Hibernate first-level cache offers repeatable reads within the unit of work. If an entity already exists in the persistence context and the application tries to fetch this entity by ID, Hibernate simply fetches this from the first-level cache and no database queries are executed. You can access all entities in the first-level cache by ID without causing any database hits if they are present.

To demonstrate this, consider the following code block:

```
Query query = session.createQuery("from Person");
List<Person> persons = query.list();

for (Person person: persons) {
  Person newPerson = (Person)
            session.get(Person.class, person.getId());
}
```

First, we fetch all the `Person` entities into the persistence context. However, later inside the `for` loop, we fetch each `Person` entity by its ID. In this case, as we fetch by the object ID, Hibernate checks to see whether this already exists in the first-level cache, and as this does exist, this will just return this entity from the first-level cache without making a trip to the database. It is important to realize that the fetch (query) and the look up via `session.get` occurred within the same unit of work.

The persistence context also checks the result set of a query execution against the cached entities. This doesn't mean that the query won't be executed. It's still executed. However, before Hibernate parses the rest of the query result, it checks to see whether this entity already exists by looking it up in the cache using the entity ID, and if it already exists, it won't process the rest of the result for this entity. The reason this is done is because pulling and keeping an entity in the persistence context requires some work, and Hibernate doesn't just maintain entities. There are lots of metadata associated with an entity that is maintained by Hibernate. So, this action by Hibernate is indeed a performance gain.

Second-level cache

In addition to the first-level cache, Hibernate offers the API the ability to utilize a second-level cache. Unlike the first-level cache, the second-level cache only stores entities that are marked as cacheable. The implementation of the second-level cache for the earlier versions of Hibernate was Ehcache; but now, Hibernate has moved to the OSGi model. Anyone can implement a second-level cache as long as they provide an implementation for `org.hibernate.cache.spi.RegionFactory`.

You can set up multiple cache regions; typically, the second-level cache has a few regions. Besides the region that stores the root entities, there are also cache regions to store collections, query, and update timestamps, which typically store only the ID of the cached entities. The region that holds the updated timestamp is used internally by Hibernate to determine whether an entry stored in cache is considered stale or not.

Typically, the second-level cache is implemented in a way that it only holds the values of entities, instead of a serialized version of each entity. (This is not a Java serialization. This may simply be a key-value map of an entity; it depends on provider's implementation.) Additionally, each value set may hold identifying references to the associated entities, which may or may not be present in the cache region. The internal of the cache implementation is vendor-specific, so this will not be discussed here. However, in this section, we will show you how to set up Ehcache as a second-level cache to work with Hibernate.

Hibernate provides support for Ehcache as the second-level cache provider, along with other providers. In order to set up Ehcache for Hibernate, you will need the following:

- Cache provider interface
- Ehcache implementation
- Cache configuration
- Cacheable entity configuration

These are discussed in the following sections.

Cache provider interface

Hibernate's interface for Ehcache is implemented in another module, called **hibernate-ehcache**, which is available as a jar, and it needs to be in your runtime class path. If you use Maven, you can simply add this as a dependency:

```
<dependency>
  <groupId>org.hibernate</groupId>
```

```
    <artifactId>hibernate-ehcache</artifactId>
    <version>${hibernateVersion}</version>
</dependency>
```

This module includes an implementation of `RegionFactory`, called `EhCacheRegionFactory`, which we'll use later in the configuration.

Ehcache implementation

The implementation of Ehcache itself (the part that performs caching functions, such as storage, access, and concurrency) is another module, which you also have to import into your project and runtime. A simple Maven dependency should take care of this:

```
<dependency>
    <groupId>org.ehcache</groupId>
    <artifactId>ehcache</artifactId>
    <version>${ehcacheVersion}</version>
</dependency>
```

Cache configuration

To configure a second-level cache for Hibernate using Ehcache, you will need to enable this in Hibernate and specify a cache region factory class by adding the following lines to your `hibernate.cfg.xml` Hibernate configuration file:

```
<property name="hibernate.cache.use_second_level_cache">
    true
</property>

<property name="hibernate.cache.region.factory_class">
    org.hibernate.cache.ehcache.EhCacheRegionFactory
</property>
```

Ehcache already comes with a default cache. However, you can further customize this. For example, you can define multiple cache regions, set a maximum number of entities in regions, and provide an expiration time for cached entities.

Consider the following example:

```
@Entity
@Cache(usage = CacheConcurrencyStrategy.NONSTRICT_READ_WRITE,
region="personCache")
public class Person {
    @Id
```

```
    @GeneratedValue
    private long id;
    private String firstname;
    private String lastname;
    private String ssn;
    private Date birthdate;
    // getters and setters
}
```

This entity is now declared as cacheable and it uses a region called `personCache`. (We will discuss cache strategy later in this chapter.) You can further configure this region in the `ehcache.xml` file:

```xml
<cache name="personCache"
  maxElementsInMemory="1000"
  eternal="false"
  timeToIdleSeconds="300"
  timeToLiveSeconds="600"
  overflowToDisk="true"
/>
```

There are other important topics when working with cache, especially a second-level cache, such as locking and transactions. We will discuss these later in this chapter. For now, let's explore query cache.

Query cache

In addition to the second-level cache, you can also enable query cache. This is especially useful for queries that are executed frequently throughout the execution of your application whose result doesn't change that often. For example, if you are writing a forum application, you can cache the result of the query that fetches the headlines of articles, as most of the time, the users are just reading the forum and if you have the list of headlines in your cache, you don't need to query the database to fetch the headlines of the articles. Of course, when a new article is posted or existing articles are updated, the query result set needs to expire or be refreshed. Luckily, Hibernate does this for us automatically. When the persistence layer commits any changes to the database in form of INSERT, UPDATE or DELETE, Hibernate will check the query cache result set. If an entity is inserted, updated, or deleted, Hibernate checks to see whether this entity is cached or could possibly be part of a query cache result set. If so, Hibernate will expire the cached data.

The query cache doesn't store entities or entity values. It only stores the ID for the entities and the values of non-entities that would be returned in the result set of the query. It uses the second-level cache to store the values of entities.

However, if the entity returned by the query is not marked as cacheable, Hibernate is forced to make additional trips to the database to fetch them. You should always examine the root and associated entities returned from a query before deciding to cache a query.

Query cache is not enabled by default. You'll have to enable it in your configuration and also when you execute the query. As query cache doesn't actually store any entities or values, it won't work by itself. So, you have to enable the second-level cache as well.

Consider the following example:

```
Query query =
session.createQuery("from Person where firstname like 'J%'")
  .setCacheable(true);
```

Let's assume that you have enabled query cache in your Hibernate configuration file, as shown here:

```
<property name="hibernate.cache.use_query_cache">true</property>
```

When the query executes for the first time, it will store the entities returned from the database and save their values in a second-level cache. Any future executions of this same query will consult the query cache first. Furthermore, if you fetch any Person by ID and this happens to be in the second-level cache, either as a result of this or another query, it will be fetched from second level cache, instead of the database.

However, if you make any changes to the persistence context after the data is cached, Hibernate will expire the cache and any subsequent queries will be forced to make a database trip.

Consider the preceding code again. If the cached query is executed again, it will not cause a database hit. However, if you delete one of the cached entities, the cache will expire:

```
Query query =
session1.createQuery("from Person where firstname like 'J%'")
    .setCacheable(true);

...

session2.delete(somePerson);

...

// cache is now expired, database hit
```

```
Query query =
session3.createQuery("from Person where firstname like 'J%'")
    .setCacheable(true);
```

Caching benefits and pitfalls

In general, the caching mechanism is designed to improve the performance of the application. This is particularly true for data that doesn't change often. Reference data is a perfect example. Another example is articles posted on a discussion forum. Of course, if this data ever changes, you would have to implement the capability to invalidate and refresh the cache. It is a general belief that your application should perform reasonably well without caching enabled. However, there are many things you could do to improve the performance and responsiveness of your application, and caching is one of those things.

However, with this added feature come pitfalls. Caching persisted data is not a good idea if the data can be modified by another application, for example, if your application runs alongside a legacy application. Another thing to watch out for is using a second-level cache in a clustered environment. Not all second-level cache implementations support clustering. Caching also increases the memory footprint of the application.

Caching is not recommended on entities that are highly transactional. The second-level cache does introduce additional overhead. So, caching entities for a highly-transactional application will not improve your performance and instead degrade the runtime efficiency.

It is important to keep in mind that most cache implementations do not actually store the entity object itself; they store the values of the object properties. This impacts the identity of the object. See the section on Object Identity in this chapter.

Every business case is different. The decision to use a cache is an architectural decision, and it requires serious assessment. It is highly recommended to make this decision by collecting metrics and monitoring your system performance.

Caching strategies

One of the most important features of a relational database is support for concurrency and how multiple users can read from and write to the database. This is known as *isolation level*. The same concept is applicable in ORM cache.

Hibernate has built-in support for various concurrency strategies and isolation levels for a second-level cache. In this section, we will discuss various strategies and when you should use one over the other.

You should keep in mind that Hibernate defines its own isolation level, but a cache provider may offer other levels. When you choose a provider, you should consult the documentation to find out what isolation levels are supported. For example, Ehcache only supports READ-COMMITTED. However, Ehcache can in fact participate in JTA transaction (global transaction) and, therefore, supports two-phase commit.

Hibernate provides an interface to access strategy for different types, such as `EntityRegionAccessStrategy`, which specifies the contract to access a cache region for entities. This access strategy defines a lifecycle for cached entities. Each cache provider must implement the APIs that are defined by Hibernate. For example, the entity region access strategy defines the interface to support the following service operations:

- `get`: This fetches an object from cache
- `putFromLoad`: This caches the object after it's loaded from the database
- `lockItem`: This locks a cached entity for update
- `unlockItem`: This unlocks a previously cached entity
- `remove`: This removes a stale object
- `evict`: This removes an object forcibly
- `insert`: This is called after an object has been inserted and while transaction is still in progress
- `afterInsert`: This is called after the completion of a transaction
- `update`: This is the same as insert, but for update
- `afterUpdate`: The is the same as insert, but for update

The concurrency strategies supported by Hibernate are defined by the `CacheConcurrencyStrategy` annotation, which can be added to a cached entity. For example, let's consider the following:

```
@Entity
@Cache(usage = CacheConcurrencyStrategy.READ_ONLY,
region="personCache")
public class Person {
    ...
    ...
}
```

We will discuss various concurrency strategies here.

Read only

This strategy is suitable for data that is almost never modified, for example, reference data. When Hibernate accesses a cache region to execute various operations, it follows a certain lifecycle that is defined by a contract. This contract is different for various strategies. For example, `ReadOnlyEhcacheEntityRegionAccessStrategy` defines the read-only strategy interface for entities in case of the Ehcache provider. Furthermore, as implied by the name, the contract is different for entities, collections, and natural IDs. The cache providers usually keep separate regions for those cache types.

The read-only strategy only supports adding and removing items to the cache. This doesn't support `update` or `afterUpdate` in the lifecycle. Nor does this support any locking. The items are added when entities are fetched from the database into the persistence context via load, and the values are not expected to be different from what is in the database.

Non-strict read write

This is slightly stricter than read-only because occasionally a *write* could happen. For example, consider the previous closing price of a stock, which is the same throughout a trading day, and which is yesterday's closing price of the stock. However, as soon as the market closes, the value that is in the cache is no longer valid and it has to be refreshed.

This strategy doesn't support locking or insert, so there is a possibility of stale data in the cache. However, as soon as an update occurs, this removes the entity from the cache region. This strategy is best for when multiple threads read the data, but there is only one thread that can update the data. For this reason, if there is a possibility of multiple threads updating the cached objects, you shouldn't use this strategy. In such cases, a read-write strategy is needed.

Read-write

When you use a read-write strategy, the cached item is locked prior to updating the values. If a lock can be obtained, the item is updated in the cache. This essentially guarantees that all threads get the committed values. So, the possibility of stale data is eliminated. However, in a clustered environment, this is not the case. Don't use this strategy when clustering because you may end up with stale data.

Transactional

This strategy is essentially read-committed, that is, bound to a managed transaction. In fact, this is the only isolation level that is implemented by Ehcache, which is fully capable of acting as an XA Resource. The latest version of Ehcache also supports this in a clustered environment. It is highly recommended that you consult its documentation.

Object identity

We discussed various cache scopes earlier, *transaction*, *process*, and *cluster*. When you retrieve a cached entity, depending on the cache scope, you may get a copy of the entity or the same instance. If you get a copy for different threads, then the two instances are equal from the database perspective, `object1.equals(object2)`, but they are not equal from the Java perspective, `object1 == object2`.

A transaction-scope cache always returns the same instance. This is because the entities are cached as proper objects, not just values. Clearly, we are talking about a first-level cache. However, a process-scope cache may choose to store only the values of entities, and every time a cached entity is requested, a new instance of the entity is created, then populated with the cached values and returned. So, you are fetching a copy of the entity. However, if a process-scope cache is implemented in a way that the entity instance is stored, then you may get the same instance for each thread. This clearly depends on the implementation of the cache provider.

Reference equality clearly doesn't apply in a clustered environment because objects are created in separate JVM spaces.

Managing the cache

Besides configuring the cache in your setting files, you can further modify the cache behavior in the code. This is important because in some cases, you would like to bypass the cache completely or force the cache to expire. We will discuss these cases here.

Remove cached entities

In some cases, you want to force the eviction of a cached entity because you may know at some of point of your program execution you will end up with stale data. You can evict entities from both the first-level cache and the second-level cache.

The API to evict entities from the first-level cache is through the session object, that is, `session.evict()`. You should note that if the cached entity has been modified during the session, the changes would not be pushed to the database when the session is flushed.

Similarly, the second-level cache provides the interface to evict a cached entity. The `Cache` class offers this API. (This used to be under `SessionFactory`, but it has been moved, so you first have to obtain `Cache` from `sessionFactory.getCache()` and then call evict.) The API to remove cached entities from the second-level cache is quite rich. You can remove an entire region by type (Entity, Collection, or Natural ID), or by region name.

Cache modes

Hibernate offers ways to modify the second-level cache behavior that is declared by your configuration settings. Setting the cache mode on the session object is the way you change the behavior.

In fact, in the same session while it's open, you can modify its cache mode as many times as you wish. (You don't have to close the session to do this.)

Consider the following code:

```
session.setCacheMode(CacheMode.IGNORE);
Person person = (Person) session.get(Person.class, personId);
...
// evict the person from first level cache
session.evict(person);
session.setCacheMode(CacheMode.NORMAL);
...
person = (Person) session.get(Person.class, personId);
```

By setting the session cache mode to `IGNORE`, the first call to get the session will cause a database hit. If we evict this entity from the first-level cache and set the mode back to `NORMAL`, the next time that we ask for the same person entity, it will fetch from the second-level cache if it's present there.

Remember that the session cache mode only affects the second-level cache. Besides `IGNORE` and `NORMAL`, there are other useful modes, which are well documented in the JavaDocs.

Cache metrics

It is important to be able to monitor the cache utilization of your application. You can collect cache metrics for further analysis. The Hibernate second-level cache API provides ways to obtain cache utilization data.

By collecting cache metrics, you can find out how many entities are put in cache regions, and how many cache hits and misses occurred. Furthermore, you can browse the content of cached data.

However, first you have to enable the generation of statistics in Hibernate and also make the cache content human readable. To do this, you would need to add the following two lines to your Hibernate configuration:

```
<property name="hibernate.generate_statistics">true</property>
<property name="hibernate.cache.use_structured_entries">
  true
</property>
```

The first line ensures that cache statistics are collected. (It also forces Hibernate to collect other statistics; we will return to this in *Chapter 7, Metrics and Statistics*, when we discuss metrics and statistics altogether.) The second line makes the cache content readable so that we can browser through it.

The cache statistics API is available through `SessionFactory`. Consider the following example:

```
Statistics secondLevelStats = HibernateUtil.getSessionFactory().
getStatistics();

// overall counts
System.out.println("stats - second level cache puts: " +
    secondLevelStats.getSecondLevelCachePutCount());
System.out.println("stats - second level cache hits: " +
    secondLevelStats.getSecondLevelCacheHitCount());
System.out.println("stats - second level cache miss: " +
    secondLevelStats.getSecondLevelCacheMissCount());

for(String regionName: secondLevelStats.
getSecondLevelCacheRegionNames()) {
  // count per region
  System.out.println("cache region: " + regionName);

  System.out.println("stats - " + regionName + ":\n" +
      HibernateUtil.getSessionFactory()
      .getStatistics()
      .getSecondLevelCacheStatistics(regionName));

  // entries per region
  Map entries = HibernateUtil.getSessionFactory()
    .getStatistics()
    .getSecondLevelCacheStatistics("personCache")
    .getEntries();
```

```
    Iterator it = entries.keySet().iterator();
    while (it.hasNext()) {
      Object entry = (Object) entries.get(it.next());
      System.out.println(entry);
    }
  }
}
```

At first, this prints the overall stats for put, hit, and miss counts. Then, for each cache region, this will print the stats for that particular region as well as the content of the cache entries in that region. You should keep in mind that some cache strategies don't provide a `toString()` method to print the entry values. The cached entities in this example are set to `CacheConcurrencyStrategy.NONSTRICT_READ_WRITE`.

Summary

In this chapter, we discussed the Hibernate cache architecture, scope, strategies, cache modes, and cache metrics. One of the reasons why Hibernate is a powerful mapping tool is its ability to reduce the number of database trips, and caching the persistent data is one of the mechanisms that help this.

You have learned about first- and second-level cache structures. You also learned about query cache. You should never rely on a cache to solve performance problems in your application. However, you should always take advantage of features that will help you achieve better performance.

The use of cached data may result in unexpected behavior in your application if not designed correctly. This chapter provided enough information to help you understand the internals of Hibernate cache. By now, you should know that if your data store is shared between multiple applications, you should not store any critical data in the second-level cache, and you should be mindful of the fact that data may be stale.

Furthermore, we discussed that special care needs to be taken with working with query cache as it may cause unnecessary database hits.

Luckily, Hibernate offers ways to configure a cache both at deployment and runtime. You should take advantage of this. You can simply set `cache.use_second_level_cache` and `cache.use_query_cache` to false and restart your application. This is helpful when you are trying to eliminate the Hibernate cache as a possible culprit for mysterious issues.

Finally, it is useless to use the second-level cache without monitoring its utilization. Collecting and generating a cache utilization report is important to ensure that your application is in fact gaining in performance when the cache is enabled.

6

Events, Interceptors, and Envers

In this chapter, we will take a look at Hibernate events, interceptors, and envers. Additionally, to understand the internals of Hibernate as they relate to some of the concepts in this chapter, we will also cover the concept of a Java **Service Provider Interface** (**SPI**) and its use in Hibernate. Events and interceptors can be triggered when we load or store entities in the persistence context. In this chapter, you will see how you can use them to implement a functionality similar to DB triggers and other event-based functions. Furthermore, this chapter covers entity auditing (envers), which implements entity revision management to automatically store historical snapshots of entities and also provides auditing mechanism. This is useful for implementing an audit mechanism in your application and allows you to implement a rollback mechanism.

- Services:
    - ◦ Service loader
    - ◦ Service registry
    - ◦ OSGi model

- Events:
    - ◦ Event listener
    - ◦ Registering listeners

- Interceptors:
    - ◦ Database trigger
    - ◦ Event or interceptor

- Envers:
  - Configuration
  - Strategy
  - Fetching revisions

Services

The concept of services is not new in Java. It is a fundamental concept that has been around since JDK 1.3, which is known as the Java extension mechanism. The idea is to make your application more *modular*, *extensible*, and *pluggable*, where you, as the developer, may provide the default behavior and also implement the capability to extend your application beyond the defaults and let the behavior change at deploy time or, perhaps, even at runtime. If you are familiar with the Spring framework, the concept of services is very much like dependency injection and inversion of control.

As you may already know, a *Service* is a published contract, a set of operations with a well-defined interface. In Java, a service can be implemented using an interface or an abstract class. A service provider offers the concrete implementation of the service. As a Java developer, you use or implement services and providers every day, and you may not actively think about it. JDBC is a good example. The API is the service interface and the underlying database-specific driver is the concrete implementation.

We will not spend too much time discussing the Service Provider Interface or the OSGi model, as those topics are beyond the scope of this book. But, we will touch on these topics on the surface so that you understand the internals of Hibernate better.

Service loader

JDK 1.6 introduced the concept of a service loader, which makes it easy to provide a service implementation. Service providers are discovered simply by looking at the `META-INF/services` filesystem location in the class path.

As mentioned earlier, most JDBC drivers follow the service provider interface as defined by the Java specification. If you explode your database-specific driver JAR, chances are that you will see a `META-INF/services` directory that includes a file called `java.sql.Driver`, which points to the specific implementation of that interface.

Service registry

Another important concept, when discussing services, is the concept of a service registry. This is the mechanism that allows your application to discover the concrete implementation of a service.

As mentioned earlier, the service loader in Java looks for implementations in the META-INF/services directory. This is similar to package scans in Spring to resolve auto-wired beans or looking up an EJB instance via JNDI.

Creating a session factory is another good example of using the registry mechanism. Prior to Hibernate 4, you could create a session factory class from the Configuration class. But, the service registry builder has replaced this because containers such as Spring and EJB can manage the session factory by providing a session service registry. For example, in a simple application that doesn't run inside an application container, you may create a session factory as follows:

```
private static SessionFactory buildSessionFactory() {
    try {
     Configuration configuration = new Configuration().configure()
         .addAnnotatedClass(Person.class);

     StandardServiceRegistryBuilder builder =
         new StandardServiceRegistryBuilder()
        .applySettings(configuration.getProperties());

     serviceRegistry = builder.build();
     return configuration.buildSessionFactory(serviceRegistry);
    }
    catch (Throwable ex) {
     // handle exception
       throw new ExceptionInInitializerError(ex);
    }
}
```

However, a container such as Spring can create and manage the session factory and wire sessions when needed. We will see more on this in *Chapter 9, EJB and Spring Context*.

The OSGi model

As mentioned in *Chapter 1*, *Entity and Session*, since version 4, Hibernate has been moving closer to the OSGi model. This model extends the idea of services one step further, in that, bundles can be installed, discovered, and removed or replaced at runtime. Furthermore, OSGi allows the tighter declaration of dependencies between services.

OSGi also implements a notification mechanism, where consumers are notified when a service becomes available or unavailable.

We can now safely discuss events and how they are implemented in Hibernate.

Events

As discussed in *Chapter 1*, *Entity and Session*, almost every action in the persistence context is translated into an event. This includes events such as `load`, `save`, `merge`, `lock`, and `flush`. For a complete list of events in Hibernate, you should look at the JavaDoc for `org.hibernate.event.spi.EventType`.

Every *event* in Hibernate has a corresponding listener that acts when the event is fired. The Hibernate event architecture uses the Service Provider Interface model to discover event listeners. This allows you to plug in your own listener for a certain event. In this section, we will show you how to write event listeners.

Event listener

Hibernate defines the event contract using the listener interfaces (refer to `org.hibernate.event.spi`) and it provides a default implementation for each event (see `org.hibernate.event.internal`). Through the service provider interface, you can append additional listeners. Keep in mind that event listeners are considered singletons, so they are not thread-safe. So, if you implement your own listener, ensure that it doesn't maintain any state.

Hibernate discovers new event listeners through another service contract called *integrator*. This is done because registering event listeners must occur when the session factory is created. If you have used older versions of Hibernate, such as version 3 or older, you may know that you needed to modify the session factory tag in the Hibernate configuration file and add your custom event listener in the event tag.

Another important note is that Hibernate gives you the flexibility to append or prepend to the existing (default) listeners or override the internal listeners. This distinction is critical. In some cases, the default listener doesn't perform any action, so you can safely override them. But, in other cases, you should always append or prepend your custom listener unless you want to override the default behavior.

Registering listeners

As mentioned earlier, all event listener operations are defined using the internal contracts defined by Hibernate interfaces in `org.hibernate.event.spi`. If you wish to write your own event listener, you will need to implement one of these interfaces. The following code shows the implementation of two event listeners:

```
public class MyPreLoadEventListener implements PreLoadEventListener {
  @Override
  public void onPreLoad(PreLoadEvent event) {
    System.out.println("**** About to load entity with ID:"
                       + event.getId());
  }
}

public class MyPostLoadEventListener implements PostLoadEventListener
{
  @Override
  public void onPostLoad(PostLoadEvent event) {
    Object entity = event.getEntity();
    System.out.println("**** Just loaded entity with ID:"
                       + event.getId());
    System.out.println(entity);
  }
}
```

The first one is called when an entity is about to be loaded, and the second one is called after an entity has been loaded into the persistence context.

Once your listener classes are implemented, you need to create your own **integrator** that implements `org.hibernate.integrator.spi.Integrator` and is used to register these listeners. Here is an example:

```
public class LoadIntegrator implements Integrator {
  public void integrate(Configuration configuration,
    SessionFactoryImplementor sessionFactory,
    SessionFactoryServiceRegistry serviceRegistry) {
    final EventListenerRegistry listenerRegistry =
```

```
        serviceRegistry.getService(EventListenerRegistry.class);

    listenerRegistry.appendListeners(EventType.PRE_LOAD,
        new MyPreLoadEventListener());
    listenerRegistry.appendListeners(EventType.POST_LOAD,
        new MyPostLoadEventListener());
    }

    @Override
    public void integrate(MetadataImplementor metadata,
        SessionFactoryImplementor sessionFactory,
        SessionFactoryServiceRegistry serviceRegistry) {
    }

    @Override
    public void disintegrate(SessionFactoryImplementor sessionFactory,
      SessionFactoryServiceRegistry serviceRegistry) {
    }
}
```

Note that the event listener registry is obtained from the session factory service registry; furthermore, the new listeners are appended to the existing listeners already registered for each event type.

Finally, for your custom integrator to be discovered, you need to add the integrator class name to a file located in your class path with the name `META-INF/services/ org.hibernate.integrator.spi.Integrator`:

In this case, the content of the `INF/services/org.hibernate.integrator. spi.Integrator` file will simply be a list of all the integrators that you wish to be discovered at runtime, for example: `com.you.package.integrator. LoadIntegrator`.

In the next section, we will show you how to achieve a similar functionality using interceptors.

Interceptors

Interceptors work similarly to events, they enable you to inject call back operations when interacting with the session. Creating and using interceptors is simpler than events. Furthermore, you can enable interceptors on a specific session, whereas events are registered globally and will apply to all sessions. But you can also enable an interceptor on a session factory, so it applies to all sessions.

Hibernate defines an interface called `org.hibernate.Interceptor` that you would need to implement. But, it also provides an empty implementation that you can extend so that you won't need to implement every method of the interface.

Most of the call back methods on Interceptor return a Boolean data type to indicate whether the method has changed the state of the entity (the state of the entity is the disassembled version of the entity properties).

When working with interceptors, you may modify the state of the entity. In that case, you shouldn't modify the entity object itself if it's being passed as a parameter; however, in most methods, the state of each entity attribute can be passed as an array, and you can modify the right element of the array. Furthermore, the names of the class attributes are also passed as a second array. So, if you need to access an entity attribute by name, you will have to traverse the property name array.

Database trigger

This section shows how to write a database trigger using interceptors.
To demonstrate this, we assume that your business contains some sensitive data, and the administrators need to track users who are looking at this data. Obviously, you would want to implement role-based access in your application to ensure that only authorized users can access the data. But, in some cases, you may want to further monitor which users are looking at which data.

We begin by create and audit entity:

```
@Entity
public class AuditTrail {

    @Id
    @GeneratedValue
    private long id;
    private String username;
    private Long entityId;
```

```
@CreationTimestamp
private Date createTimestamp;

// getters and setters
}
```

Next, we create the interceptor by extending the EmptyInterceptor class. Note that the Interceptor interface provides several methods to respond to various events, such as save, delete, and flush, and transaction events. Here, we only show an example of onLoad, but you can implement any of the methods defined by the Interceptor interface:

```
public class MyInterceptor extends EmptyInterceptor {

    @Override
    public boolean onLoad(Object entity,
        Serializable id,
        Object[] state,
        String[] propertyName,
        Type[] types) {

      if (entity instanceof Person) {
        AuditTrail audit = new AuditTrail();
        audit.setUsername(ServiceContext.getUsername());
        audit.setEntityId((Long) id);

        boolean transactionStarted = false;

        Session session = HibernateUtil.getSessionFactory()
          .getCurrentSession();
        Transaction transaction = session.getTransaction();
        try {
          if (!transaction.isActive()) {
            transaction.begin();
            transactionStarted = true;
            session.save(audit);
            transaction.commit();
          }
          else {
           session.save(audit);
          }
        }
        catch (Exception e) {
          if (transactionStarted) {
            transaction.rollback();
```

```
        }
      }
    }

    return false;
  }
}
```

There are a few things to note about the interface interceptor:

- It obtains the current session instead of opening a new session. You can certainly do this work in a brand new session, which is only recommended if you are using JTA or some other two-phase commit mechanism. That way, both sessions (the current and the session the interceptor is acting on) are within the same transactional scope, so if one fails, the other can roll back as well. Also note that this interceptor doesn't close the session. But, if you are opening a new session, you should close it.

- It's always a good idea to check whether a transaction has already started before you start a new one, in cases where you are managing transactions. Keep in mind that, if the underlying transaction mechanism is JDBC, Hibernate can only guess the status of the transaction.

- This interceptor only acts when the entity is of the `Person` type. It doesn't care about the other entity types being loaded in this session. This is done by checking the class type of the entity, using the `if` block.

- The username of the person who is fetching the sensitive entity comes from a `ThreadLocal` variable. We assume that your application sets this variable. If there are other ways in your application to identify the user who owns the request, use those.

Now, let's look at sample code that uses this interceptor. Note that we assume that, somewhere in the execution path, the username is set using the `ThreadLocal` variable we talked about earlier (in this case, this is done on the class called `ServiceContext`):

```
ServiceContext.setUsername("James");
...
session = HibernateUtil.getSessionFactory()
    .withOptions()
    .interceptor(new MyInterceptor())
    .openSession();
transaction = session.beginTransaction();
try {
  Query query = session.createQuery("from Person");
```

```
    List<Person> persons = query.list();

    for (Person person: persons) {
      System.out.println("person loaded: " + person);
    }
    transaction.commit();
} catch (Exception e) {
    transaction.rollback();
    throw e;
} finally {
    if (session.isOpen())
      session.close();
}
```

It is important to note how we are obtaining the session. In order to apply your interceptor to the session, you would need to use the `SessionBuilder` interface whose implementation is returned by calling the `withOptions()` method on the session factory. If your session is auto-wired, for example, by Spring, you can obtain the session factory from the session by calling `session.getSessionFactory()` and start a new session with the Interceptor option. Keep in mind that this will be a different session from the one Spring auto-wires.

If you write an interceptor like the previous one, you'll have to remember that this will fill up your database very quickly. You'll have to either do some cleanup occasionally or consider indexing and partitioning your audit table.

There are other use cases for Interceptors. A common one involves storing the user's password in the database. You can use an interceptor that encrypts the password before storing it in the database instead of storing the passwords as clear text. Obviously, you would need another interceptor to decrypt it.

Event or interceptor

Now that we have demonstrated both the event and interceptor mechanisms, you may wonder which is better. In short, the Event architecture is more sophisticated, but it is cleaner. Furthermore, you have access to the ongoing session and you don't have to worry about session creation or transaction demarcation. Every event type provides access to the session object with which you can interact.

The DB trigger example that we demonstrated earlier uses the interceptor mechanism. It is responsible for creating its own session and demarcating transactions. You will not have to do this with events.

On the other hand, interceptors are simpler to create and configure unlike events, which have to be registered as a service.

It's best to use interceptors for simple and straightforward tasks, and preferably not for interacting with the persistence context; instead, use events for tasks that require complicated interaction with the persistence context.

Envers

Hibernate, since version 4, fully supports entity versioning, and it's called *envers*. This is very useful for keeping track of changes to each audited entity. In this section, you will see how to configure envers, choose the right strategy for entity auditing, and handle associated entities.

Configuration

The first thing you need to do is to add the appropriate JAR and class path to your project. Hibernate envers are packaged separately, so you'll have to add the Maven dependency:

```
<dependency>
  <groupId>org.hibernate</groupId>
  <artifactId>hibernate-envers</artifactId>
  <version>${envers-version}</version>
</dependency>
```

Once you have resolved the jar dependency, you could simply add the `@Audited` annotation to the entity that you wish to track:

```
@Entity
@Audited
public class Person {
  @Id
  @GeneratedValue
  private long id;
  private String firstname;
  private String lastname;
  private String ssn;
  private Date birthdate;

  // getters and setters
}
```

That's it!

Obviously, Hibernate will let you further configure how the entity revisions are stored. We will discuss a few important configuration parameters. For a complete list, you can refer to the online documentation.

When you enable auditing on an entity, Hibernate will, by default, create a table using the entity name followed by the suffix _AUD. So, if you have an entity called Person that's being stored in the PERSON table, Hibernate will store the revisions of a person entity in a table called PERSON_AUD. (Note that, for Hibernate to create the tables, your hbm2ddl.auto configuration has to be set to create or update. If this is not possible, you can generate the schema using an Ant task. Refer to the Hibernate documentation for more information.)

By default, the audit tables contain the columns of the audited entity plus two additional columns: REV and REVTYPE. The REV column is the revision number that is incremented for every change to an entity. The REVTYPE column indicates what kind of a change occurred: the value 0 indicates entity creation, that is, insert, while 1 indicates update, and 2 indicates delete.

You can store the audit tables in a separate schema, so you don't clutter your application schema. For example, if you wish to store the audit tables in a schema called audited, add the following property setting to your Hibernate configuration file:

```
<property name="org.hibernate.envers.default_schema">
    audited
</property>
```

Obviously, the schema has to exist and the database user needs to have the appropriate permissions to write to it.

If your audited entity is associated with another entity or a collection of entities, the owned entity also has to be declared as Audited. In this case, you can configure Hibernate to create a new revision for the owning entity when owned entities are added or deleted. This is actually the default behavior. You can disable this by setting the following property in your configuration file:

```
<property name="org.hibernate.envers.revision_on_collection_change">
    false
</property>
```

Finally, it's even possible to track the changes to an entity property instead of the entire entity. This is achieved by simply annotating the property to be audited instead of the entity. In that case, Hibernate keeps track of the audited properties only.

Strategy

Obviously, enabling audit mechanism on your entities will have an impact on the performance of your application. When using envers, you can slightly control the impact.

The **default behavior** is to store a revision for each entity in the audit table along with a revision number. But, to determine when that revision was valid, another table called REVINFO is consulted; this table maintains the revision metadata. To fetch entity revisions, Hibernate performs joins and sub-selects between the entity audit table and the REVINFO table, and this impacts reading of the audit data when history is fetched.

Another strategy is to store the end revision in the audit table along with the entity data. This slows down the insertion of the audit data, slightly, but browsing through the audit history performs a little better.

To override the default behavior, set the following property in your configuration file:

```
<property name="org.hibernate.envers.audit_strategy">
  org.hibernate.envers.strategy.ValidityAuditStrategy
</property>
```

Fetching revisions

Hibernate envers offers a rich API for fetching multiple revisions of the audited entities. This is mainly done through the `AuditReader` interface. This API allows you to create queries, just like criteria objects. You can use it to fetch all revisions of entities of the same class or a specific entity, given that you provide the entity ID (refer to the `AuditQueryCreator` documentation).

For example, if you wish to fetch all the revisions of the `Person` entity, you can create an audit query as shown in the code here:

```
AuditReader reader = AuditReaderFactory.get(session);

AuditQuery query = reader
    .createQuery()
    .forRevisionsOfEntity(Person.class, true, true)
    .add(AuditEntity.id().eq(personId));

List<Person> persons = query.getResultList();

for(Person person: persons) {
  System.out.println(person);
}
```

Note that, in this case, we are filtering the entity by its primary ID. If you don't supply the ID, it will return all entity revisions of the Person class.

Another good example is using the AuitReader class to fetch the revision metadata, such as the revision number and timestamp. The following code demonstrates this:

```
AuditReader reader = AuditReaderFactory.get(session);
List<Number> revisions = reader.getRevisions(Person.class, personId);
for (Number revNum: revisions) {
  Person person = reader.find(Person.class, personId, revNum);
  System.out.println("**** revision "
      + revNum.intValue() + " at time: "
      + reader.getRevisionDate(revNum));
  System.out.println("------- " + person);
}
```

In this case, you first have to fetch the revision numbers and then look up the actual entity, using the revision number. If your entity has an update timestamp property (see the @UpdateTimestamp annotation), you can simply use the first method and order by the updated timestamp. You will see next how to order results by the entity attribute.

You can also limit the result list by setting the first result and max result, and you can also add attribute projections.

Lastly, Hibernate, by default, returns the revisions in ascending order, as it appends the SQL instruction to return the rows in the ascending order. You can, instead, order the results by a specific property of the entity. This is done by adding an order called AuditOrder to your query. You can get an instance of AuditOrder by calling AuditEntity.property("property_name").asc() or AuditEntity. property("property_name").desc():

```
AuditQuery query = reader
    .createQuery()
    .forRevisionsOfEntity(Person.class, true, true)
    .add(AuditEntity.id().eq(personId))
    .addOrder(AuditEntity.property("ssn").desc());
List<Person> persons = query.getResultList();
```

The AuditProperty API provides many additional useful methods. It is highly recommended that you look at its JavaDoc.

Summary

In this chapter, we discussed Java's SPI and OSGi model. This was necessary in order to understand the event architecture. As we saw, event listeners can be registered as services to respond to certain actions that take place in the persistence context. This sophisticated architecture empowers Hibernate to be pluggable and enables runtime environments to act as service providers.

We also discussed interceptors, which offer capability similar to events, but they are easier to create and use. The simplicity of interceptors is due to their lacking the sophisticated architecture that is used by events. For this reason, they are less modular and pluggable.

Finally, we looked at envers, which enable entity versioning and audit mechanisms. We showed that it's simple to start tracking entity revisions. But browsing through the revisions requires a bit of coding. Luckily, Hibernate envers offers a rich API to make that easy as well.

Envers uses the same event architecture that we discussed, and it is registered as a pluggable service. So, you can override it and create your own revision mechanism provided by the concepts in this chapter.

7
Metrics and Statistics

In this chapter, we will demonstrate how to produce statistical data points and collect metrics. Hibernate can be configured to start collecting and producing this data. Additionally, we will see how it can be collected through **Java Management Extension (JMX)**. We will be covering the following topics in detail:

- Statistical data types:
    - Session
    - Entity
    - Collection
    - Query
    - Cache

- Statistics via JMX:
    - An introduction to JMX

- Using JMX with Hibernate

Statistical data types

Hibernate collects various data points to help you measure the usage and performance of your application. This includes data collected about the session, entities, collections, query, and cache. Here, we discuss how to obtain this data and what each set of data points means.

To instruct Hibernate to collect metrics, you first need to enable the generation of statistical data. You have already seen how this is done in *Chapter 5, Hibernate Cache* but, just in case you skipped ahead, all you need to do is add the following property to the session factory configuration:

```
<property name="hibernate.generate_statistics">true</property>
```

Hibernate will then start collecting data points, however, be aware that this could slightly impact the performance of your application, since it now has to do more work. Later, we can see how you can enable and disable statistics data generation using JMX. You can also clear the statistics data and start over. For now, let's see what we can collect and how that is done.

Session

When you enable statistics, Hibernate collects very useful data points about your interaction with the data store. Here is a list of some of the metrics to give you an idea of what is available. You can gather data from the session factory object. For a complete list of objects, refer to the JavaDoc for SessionFactory.

Name	Purpose

Start time	This returns the session's start time. The returned value is a long value, which you can pass to the Date() constructor to create a date object; for example:
	
	``
	Statistics stats =
	        sessionFactory.getStatistics();
	Date startTime = new Date(stats.getStartTime());
	System.out.println("started on: " + startTime);
	``

Connection count	This returns the total count of all the JDBC connections made for this session factory.
Session count	This returns the total count of all sessions that were opened and closed in this session factory. There are two methods, one to obtain the open count and another for the closed count.
Entity load count	This is the total number of entities loaded by all the sessions created by this session factory.
Entity fetch count	This is the total number of lazy associated entities that were initialized because they were referenced.
Entity insert count	This is the total number of entities inserted using this session factory.
Entity delete count	This is the total number of deletions that occurred in this session factory.
Entity names	These are the entity names that were loaded in this session factory. This is useful for obtaining entity statistics by name. (Refer to the following Entity section.)
Collection names	These are the attribute names of the associated collections that were fetched in this session factory. This is useful for obtaining collection statistics by name. (Refer to the following Collection section.)

Name	Purpose
Query names	These are the attribute names of the queries executed in this session factory. This is useful for obtaining query statistics by name. (Refer to the following Query section on query statistics).
Second-level cache region names	These are the names of all the second-level cache regions used by this session factory. We saw this in *Chapter 5, Hibernate Cache*.

Additionally, when you enable Hibernate statistics, you will start seeing session statistics in your log appender every time a session is closed. This message contains a lot of information about each session:

```
INFO org.hibernate.engine.internal.
StatisticalLoggingSessionEventListener:275 - Session Metrics {
    6498 nanoseconds spent acquiring 1 JDBC connections;
    0 nanoseconds spent releasing 0 JDBC connections;
    911975 nanoseconds spent preparing 22 JDBC statements;
    9793980 nanoseconds spent executing 22 JDBC statements;
    0 nanoseconds spent executing 0 JDBC batches;
    3812324 nanoseconds spent performing 70 L2C puts;
    0 nanoseconds spent performing 0 L2C hits;
    140801 nanoseconds spent performing 1 L2C misses;
    1756437 nanoseconds spent executing 1 flushes (flushing a total of
69 entities and 21 collections);
    65969 nanoseconds spent executing 1 partial-flushes (flushing a
total of 0 entities and 0 collections)
    }
```

If that is not desired, and you still wish to collect statistics without filling your log files, you can stop this by adding an entry in your logger configuration. For example, in the case of log4j, add the following entry:

```
log4j.logger.org.hibernate.engine.internal.StatisticalLoggingSessionEv
entListener=OFF
```

Next, we'll discuss which metrics are available for entities.

Entity

In addition to the metrics you can collect about sessions, you can further collect stats for one particular entity. Note that the name of the entity is the fully qualified name, which includes the package name. You can also get the names of all entities from the session statistics, as discussed in the last section. Let's have a look at the following example:

```
String[] entityNames = stats.getEntityNames();
for(String entityName: entityNames) {
```

```
System.out.println("entity name: " + entityName);
EntityStatistics es = stats.getEntityStatistics(entityName);
System.out.println("Delete: " + es.getDeleteCount());
System.out.println("Insert: " + es.getInsertCount());
System.out.println("Update: " + es.getUpdateCount());
System.out.println("Load: " + es.getLoadCount());
System.out.println("Fetch: " + es.getFetchCount());
}
```

As indicated earlier, when reading statistics, the difference between load and fetch is that load indicates that the entity is fully loaded from the database, and fetch indicates that the entity was loaded previously in an uninitialized state, but it's now being fetched from the database to be initialized.

Hibernate returns an uninitialized object in two cases: first, if the entity is an associated entity of a parent class whose fetch mode is set to lazy, second if an entity is requested from the session via the load method. The difference between session.get() and session.load() is that get initializes the entity by hitting the database, whereas the load method returns an uninitialized proxy object and it is only initialized when the entity properties are accessed. (We covered proxy objects in *Chapter 1, Entity and Session*).

Collection

Similar to entity statistics, you can obtain further metrics about collections. Likewise, you need to get this data by referring to the collection statistics by their role name.

Query

Query statistics produce some very good metrics. This is probably the most useful data for monitoring query execution and identifying the bottlenecks. The following table shows the metrics for each query. Similar to entity and collection statistics, you'll have to obtain the query statistics by name:

Name	Purpose
Execution count	This is the number of times a query is executed.
Execution average, max, and min time	This is the maximum, minimum, and average time spent executing this query.
Execution row count	This is the total number of rows returned by executing this query since application started.
Cache put, hit, and miss count	The number of times this query added entities to cache, or read from cache, or missed when reading from cache.

Cache

We have already covered collecting cache statistics in *Chapter 5*, *Hibernate Cache*. The only thing that is noteworthy to add here is related to query statistics, discussed in the last section. It is important to note that, in order for a query to interact with cache, you need to set it to `cacheable`. So, if you expect cache hits in your query statistics, but don't find any, it's most likely that the query is not set to cacheable. In the following example the query is set to cacheable:

```
Query query = session.createQuery("from Person")
    .setCacheable(true);
```

Statistics via JMX

In this section, we will discuss how you can collect Hibernate statistics via JMX. But first, we will briefly discuss the core concepts in JMX in case you have never used it.

Introduction to JMX

Java Management Extension (JMX) was officially added to the Java Standard Edition (J2SE) since version 5. At the core of its architecture is the MBean server, also known as the JMX agent. The MBean server manages the JMX resources. These resources are called MBeans, that is, managed beans, which are used for instrumentation; MBeans provide data or perform operations. In order to interact with an MBean, it has to be registered with the MBean server first. This is typically done in the code, or if you are using Spring, you can configure Spring to do it for you. We'll see how to do this in the next section.

Finally, MBeans are accessed through a remote manager. Java2SE ships with `jconsole` and `jvisualvm` to manage MBeans and monitor VM resources. The `jvisualvm` manager has a very nice graphic interface, but it doesn't offer managing MBeans out of the box; for that, you would need to install the `jconsole` plugin.)

Each runtime environment must start the MBean server before MBeans can be registered and managed. For example, command-line applications need to be started like this:

```
java -Dcom.sun.management.jmxremote MyAppMain
```

Application servers, such as Tomcat, JBoss, and others, need to be instructed through their configuration to start an MBean server. For example, if you are using Tomcat, you need to modify the startup script, typically called `catalina.sh` (in Unix) or `catalina.bat` (in Windows), and add the following options:

```
CATALINA_OPTS=-Dcom.sun.management.jmxremote
   -Dcom.sun.management.jmxremote.port=6666
   -Dcom.sun.management.jmxremote.ssl=false
   -Dcom.sun.management.jmxremote.authenticate=false
```

You can change the port, enable SSL, and force the client to authenticate. It's highly recommended that you secure your application using SSL and enable authentication. Refer to your application server documentation for further information.

Now that we have a good introduction to JMX, let's see how we can use it to collect Hibernate statistics and perform certain operations such as enabling or disabling Hibernate statistics or resetting statistical data.

Using JMX with Hibernate

In this section, first we will see how to create an MBean to report statistical data and also perform certain operations such as enabling/disabling statistics or resetting the data. We'll also see how to register the MBean with the platform MBean registration server or use Spring to perform that function for you.

For this example, we will use a web application that is deployed on Tomcat, version 7. If you haven't already enabled Tomcat to start the MBean server, refer to the previous section to see how to do that.

If you have never worked with JMX, we recommend that you look at Java tutorials. But you may also learn by walking through our scenario, as it goes nearly step by step.

The first thing we need to do is to create the JMX managed bean. You will need an interface and a concrete implementation. In this case, our interface is as shown here:

```java
package com.packt.hibernate.jmx;

public interface HibernateStatsMBean {
 public void resetStatistics();
 public void enableStatistic();
 public void disableStatistic();
 public boolean isStatisticsEnabled();
 public String getStartTime();
```

```
    public long getCounnectionCount();
    public long getSessionOpenCount();
    public long getSessionCloseCount();
    public long getEntityLoadCount();
    public long getEntityFetchCount();
    public long getEntityDeleteCount();
}
```

The interface defines three operations: `reset`, `enable`, and `disable` statistics. It also defines attributes that can be fetched, such as the session factory start time and various counts. Now, let's take a look at the implementation:

```
public class HibernateStats implements HibernateStatsMBean {

    private SessionFactory sessionFactory;

    public void setSessionFactory(SessionFactory sessionFactory) {
        this.sessionFactory = sessionFactory;
    }

    @Override
    public String getStartTime() {
        if (sessionFactory == null) {
            return "error! session factory is null!";
        }

        Statistics stats = sessionFactory.getStatistics();
        Date startTime = new Date(stats.getStartTime());
        return startTime.toString();
    }

    @Override
    public void resetStatistics() {
        if (sessionFactory == null) {
            return;
        }

        sessionFactory.getStatistics().clear();
    }

    ...
    ...
    ...
}
```

This sample code doesn't include all the methods that are required to be implemented, but you can easily guess what they look like. You should note that this class has access to the `SessionFactory` instance. This is either injected by Spring (in my case) because Spring is managing the session factory, or, if you are managing the session factory, you will have to inject it before registering and using this managed bean.

In this case, the session factory is being managed by Spring. It is therefore better to allow Spring to declare the MBean as a Spring bean, so it can perform its own bean wiring. So, in your Spring root application context, add the following lines:

```
<bean id="hibernateStats"
   class="com.packt.hibernate.jmx.HibernateStats">
  <property name="sessionFactory" ref="sessionFactory" />
</bean>
```

Furthermore, to manage the registration of the MBean with Tomcat's MBean server, we can use a separate class. I chose to implement a Singleton and maintain the state of the registration, so the managed JMX bean is not registered more than once. Spring has a clean JMX support. Later, I can show you how to use Spring to manage MBean registration, so you don't need a class such as this. But it's good to know how this task is performed in case you don't use Spring:

```
public class MBeanManager {
  private HibernateStats hibernateStats;
  private ObjectName objectName;

  private static MBeanManager manager = new MBeanManager();

  private MBeanManager() {
  }

  public static MBeanManager instance() {
    return manager;
  }

  public synchronized void initialize(HibernateStats
    hibernateStatsBean) {
    if (hibernateStats != null) {
      return;
    }
    this.hibernateStats = hibernateStatsBean;

    final MBeanServer mbeanServer = ManagementFactory
      .getPlatformMBeanServer();
```

```
    try {
      objectName = new
        ObjectName("com.packt.hibernate.jmx:type=hibernateStats");
      mbeanServer.registerMBean(hibernateStats, objectName);
    } catch (final Exception e) {
      e.printStackTrace();
    }
  }

  public synchronized void destroy() {
    final MBeanServer mbeanServer = ManagementFactory
      .getPlatformMBeanServer();
    try {
      mbeanServer.unregisterMBean(objectName);
    } catch (final Exception e) {
      e.printStackTrace();
    }
    finally {
      hibernateStats = null;
    }
  }
}
```

Finally, we need to invoke the MBean manager at start up time. You can use a context listener to achieve this, as shown here:

```
@WebListener
public class ContextListener implements ServletContextListener {

  @Override
    public void contextInitialized(final ServletContextEvent sce) {
    ApplicationContext appContext = WebApplicationContextUtils
    .getRequiredWebApplicationContext(sce.getServletContext());

    try {
        HibernateStats hibernateStats = (HibernateStats)
          appContext.getBean("hibernateStats");
        if (hibernateStats == null) {
          System.err.println("***** null bean!!!!");
          return;
        }
        MBeanManager.instance().initialize(hibernateStats);
    }
    catch (Exception e) {
      e.printStackTrace();
```

```
        }
    }

    @Override
    public void contextDestroyed(ServletContextEvent arg0) {
        MBeanManager.instance().destroy();
    }
}
```

Note that this listener is called when Spring's web application context is started. This is needed because the `HibernateStats` JMX bean is being declared as a Spring bean because it needs access to the Hibernate session factory, which is also managed by Spring.

You are done!

All you need to do is redeploy your web application and launch `jconsole` from the command line, and point it to your server:

```
$ which jconsole
/usr/bin/jconsole
$ jconsole
```

As you can see in the screenshot, `jconsole` recognizes the local processes that are currently running. Obviously, we need to connect to the Tomcat process, namely the process called `org.apache.catalina.startup.Bootstrap`. If `jconsole` warns about the SSL connection, you can just instruct it to use an insecure connection:

Once `jconsole` is running, you can click on the **MBeans** tab and find yours, and click on **Attributes**, as shown in the following screenshot:

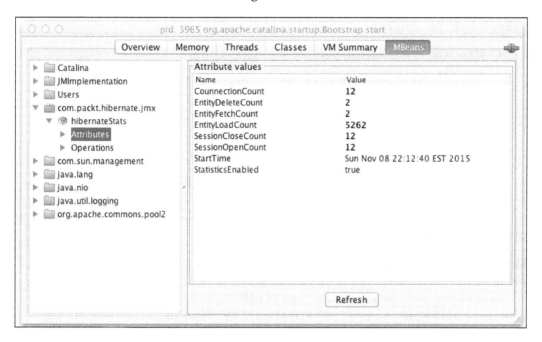

If you click on the **Operations** tab, you can see that there are buttons for reset, enable, and disable operations corresponding to the methods you implemented.

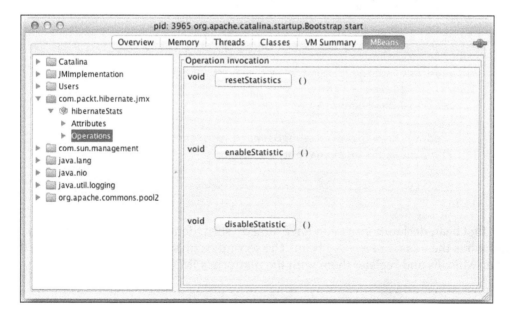

The previous demonstration used Spring to implement the solution, but again, that was only because the Hibernate session factory was being managed by Spring. The purpose of the demonstration was to introduce the components that you need to implement the solution:

- The MBean interface to define the service contract
- The MBean implementation to use `SessionFactory` to expose statistics, metrics, and operations
- The MBean manager class to register the managed bean with the platform's MBean server
- The servlet context listener to trigger the registration

So, in reality, you can do this without Spring; the only catch is that you have to safely wire the session factory object into your MBean implementation. One way of doing this is by binding your session factory to JNDI, and then simply doing a context look up for the bound object in your MBean.

However, if you do in fact use Spring, you can eliminate the last two steps mentioned here, meaning that you let Spring add your MBean to the registry server, and you don't need a servlet context listener because, in this case, Spring is the context listener. All you need to do is add the following lines to the Spring configuration file:

```
<bean id="hibernateStats"
  class="com.packt.hibernate.jmx.HibernateStats">
  <property name="sessionFactory" ref="sessionFactory" />
</bean>

<bean id="exporter"
   class="org.springframework.jmx.export.MBeanExporter"
  lazy-init="false">
  <property name="beans">
    <map>
      <entry key="bean:name=hibernateStatistics"
        value-ref="hibernateStats" />
    </map>
  </property>
</bean>
```

The first bean declaration, as you have already seen, defines an ID for the MBean and wires the `sessionFactory` bean. The second bean is Spring's bean to export the given MBeans and register them with the platform's JMX server.

Summary

In this chapter, we discussed the statistics and metrics that Hibernate can collect. We showed how you can configure Hibernate to start collecting this data and how we can get access to this data. This included datasets at the session factory level (for all sessions), including entity, collection, query, and cache metrics. Furthermore, we showed that you can collect statistics for a named entity or query.

We completed this chapter by introducing JMX and showing you how it can be used to monitor the Hibernate statistical data at runtime using a remote client such as `jconsole`. We further showed how to utilized Spring for easy integration.

In the next chapter, we'll explore architectural concerns related to enterprise applications and how Hibernate can address these concerns.

8
Addressing Architecture

In this chapter, we will discuss how to address architectural constraints for an enterprise application using Hibernate. Every enterprise application follows an architecture, which specifies the software components, such as data models, process models, user interface, and data persistence; and system components such as web servers, application servers, and database management systems. Here, we will see how Hibernate can, in fact, address some architectural requirements and constraints. The following points will be covered in detail:

- Architecture matters
- Transaction management:
    - Local transaction
    - JTA
    - Compensating transaction

- Concurrency:
    - Isolation level
    - Locking
    - Application lock

- Scalability:
    - Clustering
    - Database shards

- Performance
- Legacy application
- Cloud strategy:
    - License

- Multi-tenancy

Architecture matters

You may be able to write a simple command-line application, a utility, or perhaps even a simple desktop application without formally defining your application architecture. But enterprise applications must start with architecture, as there are many moving parts, systems, and enterprise constraints. The job of an enterprise architect is to align business goals and objectives with an IT strategy. And this doesn't only mean implementing functional capabilities, business logic, or a user interface. Enterprise architects are also concerned with non-functional business goals, such as reducing business cost and minimizing risks. Besides implementing business capabilities, application architects are also responsible for implementing the governing policies defined by the enterprise architects.

For architecture, you can use transactions to minimize data loss or to ensure data integrity, or you can scale your application to accommodate higher number of users or business transactions. There are other considerations that you need to keep in mind that are related to cost reduction. So, let's discuss some of those here and how Hibernate can address those concerns.

Transaction management

You will certainly have worked with transactions. They ensure that a unit of work is atomic, consistent, isolated, and durable. Hibernate either uses JDBC to manage transactions or participates in a global transaction, JTA.

Local transactions

We discussed session scope in *Chapter 1, Entity and Session*. As we saw, one of the options for setting the session context was a local thread. This means that the scope of the session is within the thread that is executing the code, and Hibernate will start the Transaction using the API provided by JDBC. For further information on transaction management using JDBC, refer to the JavaDoc for `java.sql.Connection`.

In the old days before Hibernate, we had to use the JDBC API to create drivers, connections, statements, and other objects to read and write from the database. Hibernate does all this work for us and more, and it still allows us to access the low-level JDBC features. For example, the implementation of *transaction savepoints* is done through the `Work` interface.

Database transactions allow us define **savepoints**, so, within the same connection, we can commit a portion of the work and continue with the rest within the same transaction. If a rollback occurs later, it will only roll back the changes up to the savepoint and not the entire transaction. Not all JDBC drivers support savepoints, but most do.

The following code shows one way of implementing savepoints in Hibernate:

```
session.save(person1);
session.flush();
session.doWork(new Work() {
  @Override
  public void execute(Connection connection)
    throws SQLException {
      connection.commit();
  }
});

Person person2 = randomPerson();
session.save(person2);
transaction.rollback();
```

There are a few things to note in the code. First, after we call the save method on the session, we call flush to ensure that the queued up actions are executed in the database. Next, we access the JDBC connection directly through the Work API to commit the transaction up to now. And, as you may notice, at the end of the work, we roll back the transaction; but, at this point, person1 is stored in the database and only person2 is rolled back.

You shouldn't have to use savepoints in most cases. This is being shared only for rare cases.

The Java Transaction API

JTA, was created to manage multiple transactional resources in one unit of work, for example, multiple databases and message queues. (JMS)

It is very common to have to read and write to multiple databases and message queues in an enterprise arena, for example, when implementing **Enterprise Information Systems (EIS)** to write to multiple databases.

JTA uses the XA protocol to allow resources to participate in a global transaction so that work can be committed or rolled back simultaneously in all systems. For this reason, the transactional resource must support the XA Protocol, and very likely you will have to use a different driver class.

 Consult the JDBC driver documentation for a specific implementation such as DB2, Postgres, Oracle, and so on. For example, the XA driver for Oracle is a class called `oracle.jdbc.xa.client.OracleXADataSource`.

JTA requires a transaction manager (JTS) that can demarcate transactions and manage all participating resources. All Java EE servers can act as JTA managers because JTA is part of the JEE specifications.

Some might think that Tomcat is a complete JEE server, but it's not. It only implements a subset of JEE specifications, such as Servlet, JSP, and JNDI. There exist JTA managers that you can run with Tomcat, for example, JOTM and Atomikos. The same people likely believe that the Spring framework implements JTA, and that is not true. Spring offers a very clean interface for transaction management but it uses the JEE application server for global transactions.

As discussed earlier, Hibernate can add a listener to global transaction events if a transaction manager exists. If you set your session context to `jta`, in the Hibernate configuration file, then Hibernate will add a `javax.transaction.Synchronization` class for receiving notifications, so it can do a session clean up, for example, flushing or discarding session data.

We discussed savepoints earlier and how to commit a portion of a transaction when working with local resources. JTA doesn't support savepoints for two reasons. Firstly, you can't commit or rollback transactions, only the JTS, that is, the transaction manager, is allowed to issue a commit because it has to perform two-phase commit. Secondly, nested transactions are not allowed in JTA. But there are ways to implement savepoints when you are in the JTA environment.

One way of doing this is to define your transaction boundaries at the JMS endpoint and let a **message-driven Bean** (**MDB**) take over the portion of the data that you want to commit regardless of what happens next in the execution path. But, you have to be aware of the fact that JMS allows you to propagate transactions all the way to the receiving MDB. You would have to configure your JMS session to reduce the scope of the transaction to the message queue and set it to auto-commit, meaning that, once the message reaches the queue successfully, the transaction doesn't propagate any further. (See the Javadoc for JMS sessions.) That way, your MDB can start a new transaction and commit the work without worrying about the rest of the execution.

Another way is to use EJBs directly and use a TX_REQUIRES_NEW handling mechanism in a CMT configuration. That way, even if you start a JTA transaction in your web application, when it reaches the EJB, the first transaction is suspended and a new transaction is started. You can commit that work regardless of what happens in the rest of the execution path.

JTA is great for making sure that enterprise resources stay synchronized. But a rogue resource can impact your application and all other resources. When working with multiple resources, pay attention to the performance of work units.

Compensating transactions

You can't always use JTA to coordinate multiple resources, for example, if one of these resources is a web service that doesn't support transaction, such as RESTFul services. In that case, you would have to implement, as part of your solution, a rollback mechanism on the non-transactional resource, or at least notify the resource that a rollback has occurred.

In fact, Hibernate envers would make a perfect solution for rolling back to a previous version of data. We discussed envers in *Chapter 6, Events, Interceptors and Envers.*

Compensating transactions are simply the Undo functionality, and in this case, the word "transaction" refers to a business transaction and not a database transaction because you are literally changing business data and restoring it to the values before the unit of work had started. A good example is canceling a shopping order because the payment was rejected further in the process.

Concurrency

Transactions offer the functionality to group multiple work units into one big unit of work, but you can further configure Hibernate to achieve better isolation in a concurrent environment. What defines concurrency parameters is transaction isolation levels as well as locking mechanisms. These concepts also require that you learn the capabilities and the behavior of the specific RDBMS that you are using because both of them are implemented by the database systems and are not Hibernate features. For this reason, you need to carefully explore the various options with your specific database system. Here, we will discuss them to show you how to control them through Hibernate.

Lastly, when dealing with concurrency issues, you'll also need to keep in mind the first-level and second-level cache, as they can play an important role in identifying problems. We discussed this topic in *Chapter 5, Hibernate Cache.*

Isolation levels

Transactions let you isolate your unit of work from someone else's work. The isolation levels allow you to draw a line between the different work units. The higher the level, the more strict the data access. Isolation is one of the characteristics of a database transaction. So, this concept only applies to one transaction while another transaction is in progress. They are listed here from the highest level to the lowest:

- **Serializable**: This is the highest isolation level. It means that, when you start a transaction, other transactions are not allowed to access the data you are accessing until the first transaction is committed or rolled back. And, if two threads try to update the same record, the first thread will succeed and the second thread will encounter an error. This provides the most privileged access to the data, but at the same time, it performs very poorly and can cause a lot of performance headaches.

- **Repeatable reads**: This means that, if you read (SELECT) data from a table and later within that same transaction you read the same data again, you are guaranteed to get the same data. While this transaction is going on, other transactions can read, but they are prohibited to write until the first transaction is completed. This performs slightly better, but it's still not good for a highly transactional system.

- **Read committed**: This is slightly better than the previous two levels. You can read as many times as you want, but it is not guaranteed that you will get the same data. This is because, between your reads, other transactions may change and commit the data. The default isolation level for most database systems is read committed.

- **Read uncommitted**: This is also known as **dirty read**, which lets you read the changes before they are committed. However, you run into the risk of reading data that may be rolled back by another transaction. On the other hand, its performance is the best because it is the least restrictive isolation.

You can set the isolation level on the JDBC connection. Hibernate lets you do this in the configuration file by setting the `hibernate.connection.isolation` property to the integer value defined by `java.sql.Connection`, where the value 1 is READ_UNCOMMITTED, value 2 is READ_COMMITTED, value 4 is REPEATABLE_READ, and value 8 is SERIALIZABLE. Let's check the following code line:

```
<property name="hibernate.connection.isolation">2</property>
```

If you are using a connection pool outside Hibernate, you can also set the isolation level in your connection pool configuration. Once you set the transaction isolation level on your database connections, in your configuration file, you can still change it for a specific session, but you'll have to do this before starting a transaction. And after the transaction is completed, that is, committed or rolled back, you should always set the isolation back to the default value, since the connection typically belongs to a pool and is reused by other threads (the connection cleanup may do this for you, but it's good practice). In this case, we use the same technique that we used earlier to access the Connection object, as shown here:

```
Session session = HibernateUtil.getSessionFactory().openSession();
session.doWork(new Work() {
  @Override
  public void execute(Connection connection) throws SQLException {
    connection.setTransactionIsolation(8);
  }
});

Transaction transaction = session.beginTransaction();
try {
  // do work

  transaction.commit();
} catch (Exception e) {
  transaction.rollback();
  // log exception
} finally {
  if (session.isOpen()) {
    session.doWork(new Work() {
      @Override
      public void execute(Connection connection) throws
        SQLException {
      connection.setTransactionIsolation(2);
      }
    });
    session.close();
  }
}
```

In this case, we set the isolation level to `Serializable` before we start the transaction. If two threads try to modify the same record, your database driver will throw an exception, which is similar to the following, for the thread that came later:

```
Caused by: org.postgresql.util.PSQLException: ERROR: could not
serialize access due to concurrent update
   at org.postgresql.core.v3.QueryExecutorImpl.receiveErrorResponse(Que
ryExecutorImpl.java:2161)
   at org.postgresql.core.v3.QueryExecutorImpl.processResults(QueryExec
utorImpl.java:1890)
   at org.postgresql.core.v3.QueryExecutorImpl.
execute(QueryExecutorImpl.java:255)
   at org.postgresql.jdbc2.AbstractJdbc2Statement.
execute(AbstractJdbc2Statement.java:560)
   at org.postgresql.jdbc2.AbstractJdbc2Statement.executeWithFlags(Abst
ractJdbc2Statement.java:417)
   at org.postgresql.jdbc2.AbstractJdbc2Statement.executeUpdate(Abstrac
tJdbc2Statement.java:363)
   ...
   ...
```

Locking

In reality, when you set the isolation level on a database connection, the database system does a good job managing concurrency. However, you can further instruct the database to do explicit locking using Hibernate to prevent data loss.

There are two types of locking strategies: optimistic and pessimistic:

- **Optimistic lock**: This strategy assumes that the data hasn't changed since the transaction began, and when you are ready to commit changes, you can safely assume that you are not overriding someone else's change. This is the behavior of the `Read Uncommitted` isolation level.

- **Pessimistic lock**: This strategy assumes that the data may change while the transaction is in progress. In order to prevent that, you can lock the record before you begin reading, modifying, and finally saving it. In other words, you want exclusive access to the data. The `Serializable` isolation level acts this way.

Hibernate lets you acquire stricter locks on an entity, which in turn translates to the SELECT FOR UPDATE and SELECT FOR SHARE statements. Most database systems support queries like this. Consider the following code:

```
Session session = HibernateUtil.getSessionFactory()
  .openSession();
Transaction transaction = session.beginTransaction();
try {
  Person person = (Person) session.get(Person.class, new
    Long(18));

  session.buildLockRequest(
      new LockOptions(LockMode.PESSIMISTIC_WRITE)).lock(person);

  person = randomChange(person);
  session.save(person);
  transaction.commit();
} catch (Exception e) {
  transaction.rollback();
  throw e;
} finally {
  if (session.isOpen())
    session.close();
}
```

In this case, two threads try to update the entity with the ID 18. Because we are requesting a pessimistic lock, Hibernate issues the following additional select query for each thread:

```
select
    id
from
    Person
where
    id =?
    and version =? for update
```

Note that the select statement is appended by for update. This tells the database that we are requesting a lock on that record. The version statement will be explained shortly. When both threads try to set the lock, the second one will get the following exception:

```
org.hibernate.StaleObjectStateException: Row was updated or deleted by
another transaction (or unsaved-value mapping was incorrect) : [com.
packt.hibernate.model.Person#18]
```

If you wish to lock pessimistically, but still allow other threads to read the data while you hold a lock, you can use the PESSIMISTIC_READ lock mode. The PESSIMISTIC_READ lock mode produces the following SQL statement; in this case, the key phrase for share is added:

```
select
    id
from
    Person
where
    id =?
    and version =? for share
```

However, two threads may not request the pessimistic read lock at the same time. To test this, let's change the code block to the following:

```
if (firstThread) {
  session.buildLockRequest(
      new LockOptions(LockMode.PESSIMISTIC_READ)).lock(person);
}
else {
  session.buildLockRequest(
      new LockOptions(LockMode.PESSIMISTIC_READ)).lock(person);
}

person = randomChange(person);
session.save(person);
session.flush();
```

This will still encounter the same exception shown earlier. (What is not shown here is the orchestration code to ensure that the first thread is really the first thread that acquires the lock.) The reason you encounter the exception is because both threads are still trying to pessimistically lock the record while allowing other threads to read the record without a less restricted lock.

There are other lock modes that Hibernate uses implicitly, such as LockMode.READ and LockMode.WRITE; you should consult the JavaDoc for additional information.

Let's talk about **version**, which we saw earlier. In order for stricter control to be enforced, you need to add a version attribute to your entity and use the @Version annotation on a column that keeps track of the entity version. This is how Hibernate detects if a row was changed since you read it and are now attempting to update it. You shouldn't let your application code modify the version number. Hibernate lets you create a version column from any data type. This is a JPA annotation. For more information, refer to the JavaDoc in the JPA API.

Explicit locking may cause deadlocks. You can set a timeout on the lock to help alleviate this. You can also ensure that the locking strategy cascades to the associated entities or nonassociated entities that may be required later in the execution path. This is usually when deadlocks occur. One thread has a lock on the root entity and another has a lock on the associated or relevant entity. Thread 1 then needs to acquire the lock on the associated or relevant entity to complete the work, but thread 2 has already acquired the lock on those entities and is waiting for thread 1 to release the lock on the main entity. So they both wait on the other, hence **deadlock**.

The database server typically detects a deadlock, and when that happens, the driver will throw an exception. So, you just have to ensure that you are catching that exception and handling the error properly.

But there is another scenario that is not quite a deadlock but could impact the performance of your application. This is the case when Thread 1 holds a lock and Thread 2 waits for that lock, but Thread 1 does not release it because it's a long running transaction. Some people refer to this as **contention**. We have already warned you that you should keep the life of your sessions short and not implement any business logic in your data access layer, such as CPU-intensive computations. If you need access to the database in between your long running logic, consider using multiple sessions and use the pessimistic locking mechanism.

Finally, if you define the association to **cascade** locks, you'll be able to further avoid a deadlock. Also, if you know in advance that you may need another entity for your data logic, you should acquire the lock ahead of time before moving forward. If you don't know what relevant entity you may need later in your execution path, then you should use a short lock timeout. This is useful when the bottleneck is not caused by a deadlock, but is rather caused by a long running thread (in Java) that is holding the lock. By setting a timeout, you are protecting your thread from other misbehaving threads. The value of the timeout depends on the code block that you are in. Use your best judgment.

User lock

At times, some developers add an extra column to indicate someone else has locked a record. In other words, the application is managing the locking mechanism. This is generally not a good idea. But if done right, it can be effective. Typically, you would write the name of the application user in the lock column and the time at which it was locked. The way a record is locked is by executing an UPDATE statement like this:

```
UPDATE customer SET lockedby = 'user1', locktime=current_timestamp
WHERE id = 100 AND lockedby is null;
```

Then, we check the row count affected by this SQL and if it is 1, then this record is now locked by `user1`.

Here are some reasons why this technique is not recommended:

- **Race condition**: This is the first pitfall; two threads execute the SQL statement and they are both able to acquire a lock. Even if you set the connection to **auto-commit**, it's still possible to encounter the race condition on some database systems. So, you most likely have to check the record again, in a new session, to ensure that you successfully acquired the lock. Some developers do this check when they are ready to release the lock. But, you can also tighten this using a pessimistic lock.

- **Stale locks**: You may end up with records that are locked by a user and then never unlocked. So, you either have to have a mechanism to be able to break a lock when obtaining one—for example, allow the users to lock the record if the lock time is more than 30 minutes. Or, if your application has a dashboard, provide admin users with the ability to unlock a record.

- **Multiple applications**: If your database is being updated by more than one application, this mechanism doesn't protect you from data loss. While you have your user lock on a record, another application may modify the record without caring if the data is locked or not. This is quite common, especially if you are modernizing a legacy application where both the modernized and the legacy application have to coexist in production, and it is most likely that you will be unable to modify the code in the legacy application. You can also work around this by checking the stored data once more before you write the changes and unlock the record.

As you can see, all this is extra work that you would have to think about carefully, and extra code and logic you would have to implement. Using user locks does bring some advantages to an enterprise application. So, if done right, it can be effective.

Scalability

Large enterprise applications that serve large number of users, without a doubt, have to be able to scale to keep up with the demand. There are various ways of accommodating scalability requirements. Let's discuss those here.

Clustering

When working in a clustered environment, you need to be aware of how it could impact Hibernate. One thing that could be impacted by deploying in a clustered environment is **identity generation**. If you use an increment strategy for ID generation even in a thread-safe mode, you are still not guaranteed uniqueness. Even if you use UUID using `java.util.UUID`, the likelihood of collision is still there, though very minimal.

Another consideration is when dealing with **detached entities**. If you keep detached entities in your HTTP session, you have to ensure that either session affinity or sticky session is enabled, or session data is shared among the nodes in the cluster. This is typically done because one of the main reasons to use clustering is to support failover, and application servers that support clustering can serialize all session data from one server to another. For this reason, any Hibernate entity that you wish to store in the session must implement the `Serializable` interface.

Finally, if you use **second-level cache** in a clustered environment, you need to ensure that the cache provider is, in fact, cluster aware. Additionally, your cache provider may use a different strategy to share cached data among the cluster nodes, for example, distributed topology, a central server serving all nodes, or synchronous/ asynchronous replication. You need to carefully consider how the use of second-level caching impacts your application consistency, data integrity, and transactions.

Database shards

The use of database shards is an architectural decision to balance database loads by splitting users and their related data into separate schemas. The Hibernate shards project was started to abstract away the complexity of dealing with multiple database schemas, most likely running on different servers. Additionally, Hibernate offers the concept of virtual shards to ease the pain of having to reshard your database structure.

Sadly, at the time of writing this, this project is still in the beta mode, but it's stable enough that there are people who are in fact using it in their production environments. The Hibernate team is working very hard to release a GA version, and now that you have read most of this book and know Hibernate pretty well, perhaps you might consider contributing to that effort.

If you would like to use or contribute to the current beta version of Hibernate Shards, you can clone the Hibernate shards project from the `git` repository, located on GitHub at `https://github.com/hibernate/hibernate-shards.git`. (Note that this URL is the current location at the time of this writing.) It's easy to build it, refer to the following commands. Once built, you can install the artifact into your local Maven repository, as shown here:

```
$ ./gradlew clean install -x test
$ cd build/libs/
$ mvn install:install-file
  -Dfile=hibernate-shards-4.0.0-SNAPSHOT.jar
  -DgroupId=org.hibernate
  -DartifactId=hibernate-shards
  -Dversion=4.0.0-SNAPSHOT
  -Dpackaging=jar
```

To generate the JavaDoc for Hibernate Shards, use the `gradlew javadoc` command after you check out the source code.

Then, simply add the following dependency to your Maven POM file to import the JAR into your project and you are ready to support database shards:

```xml
<dependency>
  <groupId>org.hibernate</groupId>
  <artifactId>hibernate-shards</artifactId>
  <version>4.0.0-SNAPSHOT</version>
</dependency>
```

The Hibernate shard project started several years ago and it hasn't kept up with the latest versions of Hibernate. But it works great with older versions. The following work was done using Hibernate version 3.6. To experiment with this, just change your Maven dependency to the older version of Hibernate:

```xml
<dependency>
  <groupId>org.hibernate</groupId>
  <artifactId>hibernate-core</artifactId>
  <version>3.6.2.Final</version>
</dependency>
```

You only have to make some configuration changes and a little code change to enable database shards. First, let's discuss how you create a shard-aware session factory.

Configuration

When working with Hibernate shards, you need a separate configuration file for each shard. This configuration file is very similar to what you have seen earlier. The following snippet shows the two additional parameters you would need to add for database shards:

```
<property name="connection.url">
    jdbc:postgresql://localhost:5432/shard0
</property>
...
<property name="hibernate.connection.shard_id">0</property>
<property
 name="hibernate.shard.enable_cross_shard_relationship_checks">
    true
</property>
```

Clearly, each configuration file has a different URL and the shard ID. But everything else pretty much stays the same.

Sharded session factory

For the sake of this demonstration, let's assume that you only have two database shards, shard0 and shard1. Let's explore the following code block that shows how to create a session factory that is shard aware:

```
Configuration configuration = new Configuration()
    .configure("hibernate.shard0.cfg.xml")
    .addAnnotatedClass(Person.class)
    .addAnnotatedClass(Child.class)
    .addAnnotatedClass(Address.class);

List<ShardConfiguration> shardConfigs = new ArrayList<ShardConfigurat
ion>();

ShardConfiguration configShard0 = buildShardConfig("hibernate.shard0.
cfg.xml");
ShardConfiguration configShard1 = buildShardConfig("hibernate.shard1.
cfg.xml");

shardConfigs.add(configShard0);
shardConfigs.add(configShard1);
ShardStrategyFactory shardStrategyFactory =
buildShardStrategyFactory();
```

```
ShardedConfiguration shardedConfig = new ShardedConfiguration(
    configuration, shardConfigs, shardStrategyFactory);

return shardedConfig.buildShardedSessionFactory();
```

As you can see, multiple configurations are created. The first configuration is used as a prototype. This is where you add your annotated classes and other configuration parameters that are not related to shards. Then, you create a separate `ShardConfiguration` method for each shard configuration file. This code block is supported by two other methods, `buildShardConfig` and `buildShardStrategyFactory`. The former is just a wrapper method and doesn't need further explanation:

```
private static ShardConfiguration buildShardConfig(String configFile)
{
  Configuration config = new
    Configuration().configure(configFile);
  return new ConfigurationToShardConfigurationAdapter(config);
}
```

The creation of a strategy factory requires a bit of an explanation:

```
private static ShardStrategyFactory buildShardStrategyFactory() {
  ShardStrategyFactory shardStrategyFactory =
    new ShardStrategyFactory() {
  public ShardStrategy newShardStrategy(List<ShardId> shardIds) {
    ShardSelectionStrategy selection =
            new LastnameBasedShardSelection();
    ShardResolutionStrategy resolution =
            new LastnameBasedResolutionStrategy();
    ShardAccessStrategy access =
            new SequentialShardAccessStrategy();
    return
            new ShardStrategyImpl(selection, resolution, access);
    }
  };
  return shardStrategyFactory;
}
```

We will discuss the various shard strategies in the next section.

Shard strategy

First, let's discuss `ShardAccessStrategy`; this strategy is used when searching for entities. A sequential access tells Hibernate to access the different shards sequentially. And, that's what is used here. A multithreaded access is also provided for supporting parallel access. The `ShardResolutionStrategy` class is used to determine a list of shards where an entity can be found. The `ShardSelectionStrategy` class is used when entities are created and stored. The following implementations are for a shard strategy based on a person's last name (Hibernate shard provides the sequential access strategy, therefore, it is not implemented here):

```
public class LastnameBasedShardSelection implements
ShardSelectionStrategy {
  public ShardId selectShardIdForNewObject(Object obj) {
    if (obj instanceof Person) {
      Person person = (Person) obj;
      String id = person.getId();
      if (id != null) {
        String[] s = person.getLastname().split(":");

    Integer shardId = new Integer(s[0]);
      return new ShardId(shardId);
      }
      // Shard ID is based on first letter of last name.
      String lastname = ((Person) obj).getLastname();
      char firstLetter = lastname.toUpperCase().charAt(0);

      Integer shardId = 1;
      // if first letter begins with letter M or prior
      if (firstLetter <= 0x4D) {
      shardId = 0;
      }
    return new ShardId(shardId);
    }

    throw
          new IllegalArgumentException("Only Person entities are
supported");
  }
}


public class LastnameBasedResolutionStrategy implements
ShardResolutionStrategy {
```

```
    public List<ShardId> selectShardIdsFromShardResolutionStrategyData(
      ShardResolutionStrategyData shardResolutionStrategyData) {
      if (shardResolutionStrategyData.getEntityName()
            .equals(Person.class.getName())) {
        String identifier = (String) shardResolutionStrategyData.
  getId();
        String[] s = ((String) identifier).split(":");
        Integer si = new Integer(s[0]);
        List<ShardId> shardIdList = new ArrayList<ShardId>();
        shardIdList.add(new ShardId(si));
      return shardIdList;
      }

      throw
        new IllegalArgumentException("Only Person entities are
  supported");
    }
}
```

Next, we'll discuss ID generation when working with database shards.

Shard ID generation

It turns out that, if we use a shard-aware ID generator, we don't need to implement the shard selection and resolution strategies. The following code shows an ID generator that is based on a person's last name:

```
public class LastnameBasedIdGenerator implements
  IdentifierGenerator,
  ShardEncodingIdentifierGenerator {

  public ShardId extractShardId(Serializable identifier) {
    String[] s = ((String) identifier).split(":");
    Integer si = new Integer(s[0]);
    return new ShardId(si);
  }

  public Serializable generate(SessionImplementor session, Object
object)
      throws HibernateException {
    // Shard ID is based on first letter of last name.
    String lastname = ((Person) object).getLastname();
    char firstLetter = lastname.toUpperCase().charAt(0);
```

```
    Integer shardId = 1;
    // if first letter begins with letter M or prior
    if (firstLetter <= 0x4D) {
      shardId = 0;
    }

    String objectID = shardId
      + ":"
      + java.util.UUID.randomUUID().toString();

    return objectID;
  }
}
```

The following code shows how to use this ID generator:

```
@Entity
public class Person {
  @Id
    @GeneratedValue(generator="ShardIDGenerator")
    @GenericGenerator(
      name="ShardIDGenerator",
      strategy="com.packt.hibernate.shard.LastnameBasedIdGenerator")
    private String id;
    private String firstname;
    private String lastname;
    private String ssn;
    private Date birthdate;

    @OneToMany(mappedBy = "parent", cascade=CascadeType.ALL)
    @Fetch(FetchMode.JOIN)
    private Set<Child> children = new HashSet<Child>();

    @ManyToOne(fetch=FetchType.EAGER, cascade=CascadeType.ALL)
    @Fetch(FetchMode.JOIN)
    private Address address;

    // getters and setters
}
```

It is noteworthy that the cascade type for the associated entities is set to ALL. If you don't do this, you will have to implement the logic to determine the shard ID for the associated entities. But, if you are directly working with the root entity, in this case Person, Hibernate can figure out the correct shard for the associated entities.

Performance

Performance is a significant architectural concern. We showed how to enable statistics in Hibernate and collect various metrics via JMX in *Chapter 7, Metrics and Statistics*, to help you identify bottlenecks. Throughout this book, we have identified ways of improving performance. Let's revisit some of these concepts here and discuss how they are effective.

Lazy loading

The decision to use lazy loading depends on specific situations. It is important to understand how lazy loading is accomplished. As we discussed, when you load an entity, Hibernate creates and returns a proxy object, which is uninitialized. (This doesn't occur when you use the `get` method.) Only when you access one of the attributes of the loaded entity does, Hibernate submit a database query to fetch the values. The same concept applies to associated entities. When you fetch the parent entities, the lazy-loaded associated entities are not fetched until they are accessed. This causes an extra trip to the database. This is an improvement in performance when dealing with one or a few entities, especially when you are not certain if you need the associated entities. But, in cases when several entities are fetched along with their associated entities, lazy loading can create a bottleneck.

It is important to keep in mind that different association types have different default fetch types. For example, the default fetch type for one-to-one and many-to-one is `FetchType.EAGER`, whereas the default fetch type for one-to-many and many-to-many is `FetchType.LAZY`.

Fetch mode

We already discussed fetch mode in *Chapter 4, Advanced Fetching*. As you recall, when you set Fetch Mode to `JOIN`, Hibernate ignores the fetch type and uses the eager strategy. However, if you fetch the root entity using HQL, it will not pay attention to the fetch mode on the association. In that case, you would have to explicitly change the HQL to fetch the associated entity eagerly, as shown here:

```
persons = session
    .createQuery("from Person p left join fetch p.children")
    .setResultTransformer(Criteria.DISTINCT_ROOT_ENTITY)
    .list();
```

Batch processing

Hibernate delays writing the data until the session is closed and the transaction is committed. If you are processing a large number of database writes, consider flushing (and clearing) the session occasionally. Hibernate is smart enough to use the JDBC batch. Besides taking advantage of JDBC batch processing, this also reduces the memory footprint of such sessions. We already discussed this in *Chapter 1, Entity and Session*.

Caching

We dedicated an entire chapter of this book to Hibernate caching. It is important to understand this mechanism very well, particularly second-level caching; it could work in your favor, or it could be the source of problem. One effective way to determine if database caching is the root cause of your problems is to turn off caching (a simple configuration change).

Stateless session

Consider using a stateless session, as it performs better in some cases. You can achieve even better throughput if you split up the work using multiple threads. But, you have to ensure that your database allows enough simultaneous connections and ensure that you have enough connections in your application connection pool. The following is an example of using a stateless Hibernate session in a multithreaded mechanism, using 4 threads to store 200,000 entities:

```
List<Thread> threads = new ArrayList<Thread>();
for (int i = 0; i < 4; i++) {
  Thread thread = new Thread() {
    @Override
    public void run() {
      try {
      StatelessSession session = HibernateUtil
      .getSessionFactory()
      .openStatelessSession();
      Transaction transaction = session.beginTransaction();

      for (int i = 0; i < 50000; i++) {
          Person person = randomPersonNoChild();
          session.insert(person);
      }

      transaction.commit();
```

```
      } catch (Exception e) {
        e.printStackTrace();
      }
    }
  };
  threads.add(thread);
}

for (int i =0; i < threads.size(); i++) {
  threads.get(i).start();
}
```

 Note that it is not recommended to spawn threads in a Java Enterprise Application. For that, you should consider using asynchronous beans. Most enterprise application servers support asynchronous beans.

Legacy application

If you are working with a legacy application, there are a few considerations to keep in mind, such as reverse engineering and modernization. Let's discuss those here.

Reverse engineering

There are times that you just want to migrate your data access from another technology—such as raw JDBC, Spring JdbcTemplate, or MyBatis to Hibernate.

The JBoss team offers a very nice eclipse plugin that provides very useful functionalities, such as model viewer, mapping diagram HQL editor, and reverse engineering. Using this feature, you can extract enough information from the database (using the appropriate database dialect) to generate Hibernate mapping files, Java classes, annotations, and more. We will not discuss the steps for reverse engineering an existing database, as clear instructions are available online. For further information, visit http://tools.jboss.org/features/hibernate.html.

We would like to share a few useful hints to help you create better maps when reverse engineering:

- **ID column**: If your database table lacks a primary key or it enforces the primary key using a unique index, Hibernate will not be able to identify the right column designated for the primary key. In this case, add a primary key or replace the unique index with a primary key; otherwise, Hibernate will create an embedded ID that will include every column of that table.

- **Composite ID**: If a table has two composite keys comprised of two or more columns, Hibernate will correctly create an embeddable to represent the ID. So, make sure that the appropriate columns are designated as primary keys.

- **Associations:** When a table column refers to another table column, ensure that a foreign key constraint exists so that Hibernate can create the appropriate associations for you. Also, the fetch types for the associations are always set to LAZY.

The eclipse plugin offers very handy features. For example, you can customize the reverse engineering file to map data types, columns, and table filters, using the provided user interface, or you can edit the XML directly.

Modernization

Often, we face the challenge of modernizing a legacy application. But, we almost never we have the luxury of suddenly shutting down the current legacy application and switching to the modernized version. For that reason, when you push the modernized version of your application to production, it has to coexist with the legacy application until the legacy version is slowly retired.

There are typically two scenarios in cases like this:

- **Two databases and two applications**: In such a scenario, both the application and the database are modernized.

- **One database, two applications**: In such a scenario, only the legacy application is modernized. The database stays the same.

In cases when both the application and the database are being modernized, besides having to migrate the data to the modernized database, you'll also have to account for the synchronization effort between the legacy and the modernized database. Some developers use the two-way **Extract-Transform-Load** (ETL) to keep the databases in sync. You can use Hibernate to push data generated in the modernized application to both databases, using events or interceptors; we discussed this in *Chapter 6*, *Events, Interceptors, and Envers*. (Ensure that you use a global transaction for this, so that, if one transaction fails, both transactions are rolled back.) However, you still have to use tools and techniques such as ETL to pull data from legacy databases. If your legacy database tables have an update column, you can write your own ETL utility and create a pull job, and use the update time as the entity version. It's highly recommended that you use a staging table to minimize the impact on application tables. Also, if you create a pull job, depending on the problem domain, you should reduce the frequency of the pulls to minimize the chances of database contention.

Another approach is to first migrate the application and then the database. In that case, you will deal with the second problem — two applications and one database. And for that, you will need to carefully examine transactions and lock strategies in both applications. In scenarios like this, you should minimize the use of cached data. You can still cache data that is never or rarely modified.

The Cloud strategy

Cloud deployment is more popular than ever. Nowadays, most enterprise applications are designed to run either on-premise or in the cloud. You can create an application that offers the same services to different clients, while isolating the client data from each other. There are several motivational factors behind this strategy and one of those is to save licensing costs. This is common when creating **Software-as-a-Service (SaaS)**.

Licensing

In a cloud architecture, you only use and pay for the things that you need. You can create an application that only requires a database, and you don't need content management, image processing, message queuing, or other services. Even if you deploy on-premise, some vendors offer licensing models to enable features only if you pay for them.

Furthermore, some application servers and database vendors charge per instance or even per schema. You can use various techniques to reduce your cost so you don't have to pay the additional fee, one is multi-tenancy, and Hibernate offers the tools to implement it.

Multi-tenancy

When you create an application and offer it as a service, you can deploy it on premise and charge your customers individually, or you can deploy it in the cloud and reduce the cost and maintenance fees for your clients. However, you will still have to isolate the client data from each other.

There are three ways of making a multi-tenant application:

- One application, multiple databases
- One application, one database, multiple schemas
- One application, one database, one schema

The first two are implemented using a multi tenant connection provider, which maintains multiple connection pools for multiple databases, or one connection pool for multiple schemas hosted on the same database. Some database drivers don't support the latter, in which case, you are forced to use multiple connection pools for different schemas on the same database instance.

The last model is implemented in such a way that each table in the schema has a tenant ID associated with it, and Hibernate composes the SQL queries while being aware of the multi-tenant model. This feature is not fully implemented yet but should be available in future releases of Hibernate.

Summary

In this chapter, we discussed several different topics that address architectural concerns, all of which are important topics. Using transactions, you can ensure that the data in your unit of work is persisted correctly, and you can tighten the concurrency boundaries by setting the appropriate parameters, such as isolation levels and database locks. We also discussed compensating transactions to implement the undo functionality, and we covered using custom user locks to offer application users more control over the data.

We showed what to watch for when your application is deployed in a clustered environment and also how to implement an application using multiple database shards. Even though, throughout this book, we have discussed performance concerns, we further addressed other concerns related to performance in this chapter.

We also discussed how to reverse engineer a legacy application and the approaches to modernization efforts. And finally, we discussed licensing concerns, multi-tenancy, and how Hibernate can address this issue.

In the next chapter, we will discuss how to configure Hibernate to work in the Spring context as well as the EJB context.

9
EJB and Spring Context

In this chapter, we will discuss how to integrate Hibernate in two popular contexts, EJB and Spring. The EJB context is part of the **Java Enterprise Edition (JEE)** specifications, and Spring is an open source context that is highly popular because it simplifies working in a JEE environment by adding a thin layer.

- Deployment:
    - Configuration
    - Resource
    - Transactions
    - Hibernate libraries

- EJB:
    - Persistence unit
    - Server resources
    - Entity manager
    - Transactions

- Spring:
    - Configuration
    - Transaction management
    - Data source
    - Session factory

Deployment

When deploying an application that uses Hibernate, you will most likely have to perform configuration steps to complete the deployment. This is because, in various contexts, the application server or the container manages the resources that are needed for runtime. In this section, we will discuss some of those topics, and later we will see how to complete these steps in the EJB and Spring contexts, as they are different.

 Throughout this book, and particularly in this chapter, the terms *context* and *container* are mostly used interchangeably. These terms are used to refer to EJB, Servlet, and Spring containers. The term *application server* refers to the runtime platform for your Java enterprise application, for example, JBoss or WebLogic.

Configuration

In both the EJB and Spring context, it is best, and sometimes mandatory, to give the container/context manage the necessary resources. For this reason, you would need to use the context configuration files to set up resources for Hibernate. You can use the typical Hibernate configuration file to create resources and set configuration parameters, however, in order for the container to be aware of these configuration parameters and manage resources properly, they will have to reside in configuration files that are known to the container.

For example, you need to pass complete control of the Hibernate session to the container because, most likely, it is the container that manages resources such as the database connection pool, transactions, and dependency injection. The specifics of the configuration settings will be shown for both EJB and Spring.

Resource

The job of containers and application servers is to manage resources that are needed by an application to reduce the complexity of deployment and management. Some examples of resources are thread pools, database connection pools, the JNDI naming service, service end points, and message queue connection factories.

When using Hibernate in an application server, you should delegate the work of database connection management and transaction management to the container.

Transaction

The JEE includes specification for **Java Transaction API (JTA)**, and all JEE application servers, such as WebLogic, WebSphere, and JBoss, implement this specification. This is designed to orchestrate the atomic work between the various transactional resources, such as multiple Databases, Message Queues, and any other resource that implements the XA protocol, which is the protocol to achieve a two-phase commit strategy.

The original JDBC specification didn't include support for XA. But, JDBC 2.0 has been extended to provide this support through the `javax.sql.XAConnection` and `javax.sql.XADataSource` APIs.

Most enterprise applications do require coordination between multiple transactional resources. So, it is very likely that you will need to use JTA. For this reason, when you configure the JDBC and JMS drivers for your application server, make sure that you use the XA version of the drivers.

As discussed earlier, Hibernate is fully aware of JTA and prefers it; all you have to do is tell Hibernate that its session is contained within the scope of a JTA transaction.

Hibernate libraries

Hibernate features and capabilities are packaged in libraries, and, in the case of Java, they are made available in various JARs. Some application servers, such as JBoss, include these libraries in the application server stack because they use Hibernate as their JPA implementation, which is why there is no need to include Hibernate JARs in your application **Enterprise Archive (EAR)** or **Web Application Archive (WAR)**.

If you do include the Hibernate JARs in your deployable artifacts, you may run into issues because you may have a version of Hibernate that is not compatible with the other runtime libraries. It's best to work with your system engineer to patch JBoss to include the latest version of Hibernate because you may also have to upgrade other JBoss libraries to make sure that they are compatible.

When deploying your application on other application servers, such as WebLogic, Glassfish, or WebSphere, you can package Hibernate libraries inside your application EAR and let the application server know that you wish to use Hibernate as your JPA implementation. Alternatively, you can drop those libraries in the application server stack so that they can be used by other Hibernate applications running on the same server.

If you are using Maven and you decide not to include Hibernate JARs in your deployable artifact because they already exist in the server's class path, simply change the scope of the Hibernate dependencies to provide. This way, the libraries are available during development, but when you create the build artifacts, they will not be packaged.

EJB

If you ever created an EJB application using older versions of JEE specifications, J2EE, you would remember that data persistence was achieved using Entity Beans, which implemented the `javax.ejb.EntityBean` interface, and you had to implement all those horrifying methods and provide different implementations, depending on the persistence nature of the entity bean, that is container-managed or bean-managed.

Thanks, mostly, to Hibernate, the **Java Persistence API (JPA)** was born to simplify the implementation. In the next section, we will see how to set up Hibernate as the entity manager when using EJB 3.

Persistence unit

In the JPA world, the Entity Manager represents the persistence unit. It is defined by the `javax.persistence.EntityManager` interface. This is the JPA API that is your gateway to the persistence store, just as the Hibernate Session is when working directly through the Hibernate API. In EJB3, you will need to declare the persistence unit and let the application server know who the provider is if you wish to override the provided implementation.

The persistence unit is declared in a file called `persistence.xml`, located in the `META-INF` directory. Here is a sample that tells the EJB container to use Hibernate as the JPA provider. It also tells the container that you wish to use JTA for transaction management. Let's check the following example:

```xml
<?xml version="1.0" encoding="UTF-8"?>
<persistence version="2.1"
  xmlns="http://xmlns.jcp.org/xml/ns/persistence"
  xmlns:xsi="http://www.w3.org/2001/XMLSchema-instance"
  xsi:schemaLocation="http://xmlns.jcp.org/xml/ns/persistence
  http://xmlns.jcp.org/xml/ns/persistence/persistence_2_1.xsd">
  <persistence-unit name="MasteringHibernate"
    transaction-type="JTA">
    <provider>org.hibernate.ejb.HibernatePersistence</provider>
```

```
    <jta-data-source>java:jboss/datasources/postgresDS</jta-data-
        source>

    <class>com.packt.hibernate.ch9.model.Person</class>
    <class>com.packt.hibernate.ch9.model.Child</class>

    <properties>
        <property name="hibernate.dialect" value="org.hibernate.dialect.
PostgreSQLDialect" />
        <property name="hibernate.hbm2ddl.auto" value="update" />
        <property name="hibernate.show_sql" value="true" />
        <property name="hibernate.format_sql" value="true" />
    </properties>
  </persistence-unit>
</persistence>
```

This is also where you declare the entity classes. As can be seen, you can include in-container, provider-specific properties—in this case, the Hibernate dialect and other properties.

Server resources

As we saw in the previous section, the only resource that needs to be configured in the persistence unit is the JTA data source. But, behind the scenes, your application server has to provide the JDBC driver, create a connection factory, and manage transactions, and all of that requires configuration and management on the server side. However, such tasks are beyond the scope of this book as they are specific to each application server.

For the sake of demonstration, we will briefly discuss these steps here using JBoss AS 7 and PostgreSQL as the database.

You can specify the connection information, set up the database driver, and configure a connection pool in your JBoss configuration file, as shown in the following code snippet.

 If you are using the simple standalone version of JBoss, this configuration file is called `standalone.xml` and is located in the directory called `/standalone/configuration`, under the JBoss directory.

Note that the data source is registered as a JNDI resource, which is used by the persistence unit we saw earlier:

```
<datasource jta="true" jndi-name="java:jboss/datasources/postgresDS"
        pool-name="postgresDS" enabled="true" use-java-context="true"
use-ccm="false">
        <connection-url>jdbc:postgresql://localhost:5432/packtdb</
connection-url>
        <driver-class>org.postgresql.Driver</driver-class>
        <driver>postgresqlDriver</driver>
        <pool>
            <min-pool-size>5</min-pool-size>
            <max-pool-size>100</max-pool-size>
            <prefill>true</prefill>
        </pool>
        <security>
            <user-name>dbUser</user-name>
            <password>password</password>
        </security>
    </datasource>
    <drivers>
        <driver name="postgresqlDriver" module="org.postgresql">
            <xa-datasource-class>org.postgresql.xa.PGXADataSource</xa-
datasource-class>
        </driver>
    </drivers>
</datasources>
```

Furthermore, note that this data source is set up as a JTA resource and the driver class used for this data source is the XA flavor. Finally, the module that contains the PostgreSQL drivers is called `org.postgresql`, as shown in the earlier example.

 JBoss uses modules to extend its capabilities. In fact, Hibernate is added as a module. So, if you need to upgrade Hibernate, look for its module and upgrade the JARs there. Refer to the JBoss documents for more information.

To add your database driver to JBoss as a module, create a directory under the JBoss module's directory, copy the JARs to the new directory,, and create a file called `module.xml` to tell JBoss about the new module. The name of the module directory is very important. Since the module is called `org.postgresql`, the directory must be called `org/postgresql/main`. The contents of this directory are shown here:

```
$ pwd
/opt/jboss-as-7.1.1/modules/org/postgresql/main
```

```
$ ls
module.xmlpostgresql-9.4.jar          postgresql-9.4.jar.index

$ cat module.xml
<?xml version="1.0" encoding="UTF-8"?>
<module xmlns="urn:jboss:module:1.1" name="org.postgresql">
    <resources>
        <resource-root path="postgresql-9.4.jar"/>
    </resources>
    <dependencies>
        <module name="javax.api"/>
        <module name="javax.transaction.api"/>
    </dependencies>
</module>
```

The index file is created by JBoss; after you restart it, it will discover this new module and create an index file.

Now, you are ready to start using Hibernate.

Entity manager

In this section, we will discuss how to work with the entity manager in a session bean. So far, we have been working with Hibernate sessions, and most of the examples used to demonstrate the concept were for a standalone application.

But when you use Hibernate in an EJB context, things are a little different. First, let's recognize the choice that you have between using the JPA interface, that is the entity manager, and the Hibernate interface, that is a session. Throughout this book, we have mostly covered Hibernate sessions. But, for now, we will focus mostly on the entity manager.

When you declare your persistence unit, as shown earlier, you can simply inject it in your session bean, using the annotation @PersistenceContext. Consider the following example:

```
@Stateless(name="personBean")
public class PersonBean implements PersonDAO {
  @PersistenceContext(unitName = "MasteringHibernate")
  private EntityManager entityManager;

  @Override
  public Person findById(long id) {
    return entityManager.find(Person.class, id);
  }
```

```
    @Override
    public List<Person> findAll() {
      List<Person> persons =
              entityManager.createQuery("from Person", Person.class)
              .getResultList();
      return persons;
    }

    @Override
    public void save(Person person) {
      entityManager.persist(person);
    }

    @Override
    public void update(Person person) {
      entityManager.merge(person);
    }

    @Override
    public void delete(long id) {
      Person person = entityManager.find(Person.class, id);
      if (person == null) {
        throw new RuntimeException("Object not found!");
      }
      for(Child child: person.getChildren()) {
        delete(child);
      }
      delete(person);
    }

    @Override
    public void delete(Object entity) {
      entityManager.remove(entity);
    }
  }
```

The first thing to notice is the auto-wired persistence context. Once you declare your persistence unit in the `persistence.xml` file, you can inject it in your EJBs (a stateful/ stateless session and a message-driven bean), as shown in the preceding example.

 You can also look up the persistence unit, using a JNDI context lookup. But, when working with EJBs, there is no need to do that; just use an annotation.

The rest of the example comprises simple data access methods using the entity manager API. There seems to be something missing! What about a transaction? Let's discuss that next.

Transaction

In the example shown in the previous section, we didn't declare any transactional attributes or demarcate a transaction. There are two reasons for this. First, by default, the EJB container manages transactions for the beans. Second, every EJB method, by default, requires a transaction. So, if you don't provide any transactional attribute, the container will create a transaction before invoking the EJB method, if one doesn't already exist. By default, transactions propagate across different methods in the same execution path.

You can specify different transaction attributes per EJB specifications. For example, if an EJB method should run in its own transaction, you can annotate the method using `@TransactionAttributeType.REQUIRES_NEW` to suspend the current transaction and start a new one.

The scope of the entity manager is set to the transaction. This means that, once the transaction commits, the entity manager is flushed and closed.

If the EJB, and not the container, manages your transaction, you are responsible for starting and committing the transaction in your EJB method. For further information on this, refer to the Java enterprise documentation, as EJBs are beyond the scope of this book.

Hibernate session

When working with EJBs while using Hibernate as the JPA implementation, you can still access the Hibernate Session. Throughout this book, we have already pointed out a few things you can do with Hibernate Session that are not offered through JPA interface. So, there might be scenarios under which you would need to access the `Session` object.

You can access the underlying session by asking the entity manager to provide the underlying implementation. For example, you can replace the `find` method, shown in the earlier example, to use the Hibernate session. The Hibernate session is obtained by calling the `unwrap` method on the entity manager API:

```
@Override
public Person findById(long id) {
  Session session = entityManager.unwrap(Session.class);
  return (Person) session.get(Person.class, id);
}
```

If you use JBoss, you can in fact use the Hibernate session as your entity manager.

```
public class PersonBean implements PersonDAO {
  @PersistenceContext(unitName = "MasteringHibernate")
  private Session session;
  ...
}
```

Clearly, this will not work in EJB containers other than JBoss.

Spring

Spring is another popular context that is used by many Java developers because it simplifies application development by offering capabilities such as dependency injection and **aspect-oriented programming (AOP)**. Spring is a lightweight context, but it doesn't implement the JEE specifications, so it's not a Java enterprise container.

 Spring used to be known simply as a context, but the current direction of Spring is, in fact, moving towards being a standalone container, so enterprise applications can be written without having to implement JEE specifications. Spring now offers a Model-view-controller framework, web services, Spring data, batch, Spring integration, and many other capabilities, which collectively make Spring a worthy competitor to JEE. Nevertheless, Spring plays very nicely in JEE containers while simplifying many configuration and deployment tasks.

In this section, we will discuss how to configure Hibernate using the Spring container. If you are new to Spring, we highly recommend that you refer to the user guides available online.

Configuration

In a typical Spring application, the Hibernate session factory is declared as a Spring bean, which is then injected into various **Data Access Objects. (DAO)** classes. Furthermore, this allows you to inject other resources, such as a data source and transaction manager, into the Hibernate session factory. To declare the Hibernate session factory as a Spring bean, you'll have to use a wrapper class, as shown here:

```
<bean id="sessionFactory"
  class="org.springframework.orm.hibernate4.LocalSessionFactoryBean">
    <property name="dataSource" ref="dataSourceJndi" />
    <property name="jtaTransactionManager" ref="transactionManager"/>
    <property name="configLocation"
```

```
                    value="classpath:hibernate-spring.cfg.xml" />
        <property name="packagesToScan"
                    value="com.packt.hibernate.ch9.model" />
    </bean>
```

The wrapper class is included in the Spring ORM library, which includes support for different versions of Hibernate. Another thing to note is that we will use a data source that is configured by the app server. You can declare the data source bean, like this:

```
<jee:jndi-lookup id="dataSourceJndi"
        jndi-name="java:jboss/datasources/postgresDS"/>
```

Also, note that, for this example, we will use the JTA transaction manager provided by the app server, which can be declared like this:

```
<bean id="transactionManager"
    class="org.springframework.transaction.jta.JtaTransactionManager"/>

<tx:jta-transaction-manager
    transaction-manager="transactionManager"/>
```

The Hibernate entities can be discovered by the **packagesToScan** property. And finally, you can declare additional Hibernate properties in a separate configuration file and allow Spring to further configure Hibernate using that file. This property is the typical configuration file that you would use with a standalone Hibernate application:

```
<?xml version='1.0' encoding='utf-8'?>
<!DOCTYPE hibernate-configuration PUBLIC
        "-//Hibernate/Hibernate Configuration DTD 3.0//EN"
        "http://www.hibernate.org/dtd/hibernate-configuration-
3.0.dtd">
<hibernate-configuration>
  <session-factory>
    <property
            name="dialect">org.hibernate.dialect.PostgreSQLDialect</
property>
    <property name="hbm2ddl.auto">update</property>
    <property name="current_session_context_class">jta</property>
    <property name="show_sql">true</property>
    <property name="format_sql">true</property>
  </session-factory>
</hibernate-configuration>
```

Transaction management

When working with Spring, you can decorate your service methods (or DAO methods) with the `@Transactional` annotation to demarcate transactions. Spring will then participate in a global transaction and commit or rollback accordingly.

In the case of global transactions, the transaction coordinator (typically, the application server) manages the life cycle of a transaction. Spring is still at the mercy of JTA because of the two-phase commit; when multiple transactional resources are part of the unit of work, the transaction coordinator will decide to commit or roll back the global transaction.

However, Hibernate also needs to know about the transaction manager because Hibernate Session requires a transactional context. This is facilitated by Spring. The `transactionManager` Spring bean, which we saw earlier, is responsible for discovering the provided JTA manager, and that is done through the JNDI lookup. And as you saw, this transaction manager bean is wired to the Hibernate session factory through the session factory wrapper.

If you are using a local transaction, Spring can still begin and commit/rollback transactions for you. In that case, simply change the transaction manager to the local transaction, shown here:

```
<bean id="transactionManager"
  class="org.springframework.orm.hibernate4.
HibernateTransactionManager">
  <property name="sessionFactory" ref="sessionFactory" />
</bean>
```

Data source

The configuration example shown earlier, uses the data source and connection pool that is configured on the application server. If the application server does not manage the data source, Spring can create and manage one for your application. An example is shown here:

```
<bean id="myDS" class="org.apache.commons.dbcp2.BasicDataSource"
        destroy-method="close">
  <property name="driverClassName" value="org.postgresql.Driver" />
  <property name="url"
      value="jdbc:postgresql://localhost:5432/packtdb" />
  <property name="username" value="dbuser" />
  <property name="password" value="password" />
</bean>
```

Session factory

Working with Hibernate session in the Spring context is similar to working with Entity Manager in the EJB context. However, Spring can only wire the session factory class, you still need to obtain a session from the factory.

A typical DAO class may look like the one shown here:

```
public class PersonDAOImpl implements PersonDAO {
    private SessionFactory sessionFactory;

    public PersonDAOImpl(SessionFactory sessionFactory) {
        this.sessionFactory = sessionFactory;
    }

    @SuppressWarnings("unchecked")
    @Override
    @Transactional
    public List<Person> list() {
        return sessionFactory.getCurrentSession()
                .createCriteria(Person.class)
                .addOrder(Order.asc("id"))
                .setResultTransformer(Criteria.DISTINCT_ROOT_ENTITY)
                .list();
    }

    @Override
    @Transactional
    public Person findById(long personId) {
        return (Person) sessionFactory.getCurrentSession().get(Person.
class, personId);
    }

    @Override
    @Transactional
    public void save(Person person) {
        sessionFactory.getCurrentSession().save(person);
    }

    @Override
    @Transactional
    public void update(Person person) {
        sessionFactory.getCurrentSession().saveOrUpdate(person);
    }
```

```
    @Override
    @Transactional
    public void delete(long personId) {
        Person person = (Person) sessionFactory.getCurrentSession().
get(Person.class, personId);
        sessionFactory.getCurrentSession().delete(person);
    }
}
```

The first thing to note is that the session factory is provided by Spring through dependency injection. In your Spring configuration file, you will need to declare this class as a Spring bean and then wire in the session factory, as shown here:

```
<bean id="personDao" class="com.packt.hibernate.dao.PersonDAOImpl">
  <constructor-arg>
    <ref bean="sessionFactory" />
  </constructor-arg>
</bean>
```

Next, note that the methods of this DAO class are annotated as `transactional`. When Spring encounters this, it will ensure that a transaction has started before calling this method.

> Typically, a Spring application has a *Service* layer and a *DAO* layer. The service layer is where the business logic is implemented, and within that logic, you may need to connect to multiple transactional resources, and each service method is typically considered a unit of work. This is why the transaction is demarcated in the service layer, so you will annotate the service method as `transactional` and that transaction will propagate to the DAO layer. This example doesn't have a service layer since it's a simple **Create, Read, Update, Delete (CRUD)** application.

Finally, note that you still have to obtain a session from the session factory because what is injected is the factory class.

Summary

In this chapter, we discussed how to prepare the deployment of our Hibernate application in the EJB and Spring context. Enterprise application deployment is not always an easy task. However, we identified the things that you should keep in mind when deploying in a container. You will need to use the configuration files that are recognized by the containers and application servers, such as `persistence.xml`. Also, you should delegate the task of resource management to the container or the application server. For example, it's always a good idea to let the container manage database connection pools and just access it as a data source. Transaction management is also another concern that is best left to the container.

Both EJB and Spring do a good job at providing a runtime context to simplify the deployment and management of your runtime application.

We discussed how to write an EJB class that uses the JPA entity manager and how transactions are managed in the EJB context. We also discussed how to achieve the same goals using the Spring context.

I hope you enjoyed reading this chapter and this entire book. More importantly, I hope that this book helps you write better applications using Hibernate.

Index

Symbols

A